THE ~~BLACK~~ FUTURE OF MONEY

ALEX HERNANDO

© 2024, Alex Hernando

All rights reserved. No part of this publication may be reproduced, distributed or transmitted in any form or by any means, including photocopying, recording or other electronic or mechanical methods, without the prior written permission of the copyright holder, except in the case of brief quotations cited in critical reviews and other activities permitted by copyright law.

All images and graphics used in this book are the property of the author and/or have been used with permission. Unauthorized reproduction or use of these images and graphics is strictly prohibited.

For permission to reproduce, please contact Alex Hernando at elfuturonegrodeldinero@gmail.com.

CONTENTS:

ABOUT ME ....
SYNOPSIS ....
SURPRISE AWARD ....

1. LET'S GET INTO THE SITUATION 1

    Introduction to the world of cryptocurrencies & CBDCs 1

    A financial revolution 5

    Key definitions 10

2. GETTING DOWN ON BUSINESS 166

    What is a CBDC? 166

    Are all CBDCs the same? 17

    Main features of CBDCs? 233

    Where do CBDCs come from? 266

    What are they really for? 28

3. LET'S GO DEEPER 400

    What about the companies? 40

    Are CBDCs good or bad? 42

    Where are we heading? 46

    Current CBDC projects 48

4. ARE THEY GOING TO AFFECT US? 69

    What improvements do CBDCs really offer? 69

    Can CBDCs harm us economically? 72

    What about laws? 77

    So, it can be risky, can't it? 78

    A real project from the inside - Britcoin 84

5. HATEFUL COMPARASIONS 94

    Differences between CBDCs and cryptocurrencies 94

    Differences between CBDCs and stablecoins 98

    Differences between CBDCs and current money 100

6. PERSONAL REFLECTIONS 106

    What I should do now? 106

    Alex, what's your opinion? 108

NOTES 112

ABOUT ME

I am sure you are wondering, as usual, who is the author of this book, so let me introduce myself. My name is Alex Hernando, and I am a young man born in 2000 in Catalonia and with a financial background and above all very proactive. I am also a **financial advisor qualified** with the MIFID II

I was a **semi-professional sportsman** for several years and this has helped me to create a mentality and discipline that I believe is one of my greatest strengths...

Once I finished my time as an elite athlete, I started a degree in Accounting and Finance, where I discovered something that I loved in the mention of finance and, as a reward, I got the extraordinary prize for the **best academic record of my degree**.

In addition, I am a member of the college of economists of Catalonia, and, despite my young age, I have already attended lectures even as a speaker in front of people with important positions such as the mayor of Girona and others.

I have never stopped training, especially in personal finance, blockchain and cryptocurrencies, so in this book we will take a journey into an event that, in my opinion, is going to change the global financial system and we still don't seem to know about it.

If you want to know more about me or need anything else, do not hesitate to contact me through my LinkedIn profile.

 Alex Hernando

SINOPSIS

Think CBDCs are just another boring digital currency? Nothing could be further from the truth! This book will effortlessly take you to understand what central bank digital currencies are and believe me whoever you are you need to understand what they are and why they are going to be so important in the times to come. And you don't need to be an ace economist!

Most people don't know it, but in the next few years we are going to experience a change in the world economy, remember the change from the peseta to the euro? Well, something even bigger is coming and people don't seem to know it! You will dive into amazing projects you may have never heard of and discover why central banks around the world are so in love with CBDCs.

Do you know what the main CBDC projects are and what uses they are being put to?

You will probably not know the answer, but you will be surprised by the number of countries that already have projects in place and the importance they are already gaining.

On the other hand, like everything in life, it is very important to know why, that is to say, ¿ **What is the real reason why most central banks are implementing their own CBDC?**

Don't worry, throughout the book you will know the answer to this and many more questions, and I bet that after this book you will see the economy and CBDCs in a completely different light!

Is a CBDC the same as a cryptocurrency? Well, the reality is that they are very different! In fact, we could consider them as the hero and the villain, but I won't reveal which one is the hero and which one is the villain, you will have to find out for yourself as you read on.

In addition, I will not only explain many things about them, but I will also explain the risks involved and how we can play chess to avoid them.

Finally, I propose a challenge:

The challenge is to answer a question first before reading the book and then once you have read it. The question is as follows:

Do you think CBDCs will really be implemented?

FIRST ANSWER (BEFORE TO READ THE BOOK):

SECOND ANSWER (AFTER):

Whatever your final answer is, I'd appreciate it if you'd let me know by leaving me a review through Amazon, as I'm interested to know what people like you think about CBDCs and about my book!

SURPRISE AWARD

Dear reader, you may not know this, but, among other things, I provide financial coaching services. You are probably wondering, what is that? Well, it's simple, broadly speaking, I provide the following services:

I help you to manage and improve your personal finance.

> Financial Goals
>
> Debt and expense management.
>
> Insurance and financial protection.
>
> I motivate and support you by providing tips and financial education to help you achieve your goals.
>
> Advice on portfolio management and retirement planning.

Why am I telling you this? Because, to thank you for your reading and support, I am going to give you a free one-hour session with me to analyze your financial situation and see how we can improve it.

I ask only one favor in return:

You must write a review of this book on Amazon and recommend this book to two people, send me a screenshot of the review and recommendations at elfuturonegrodeldinero@gmail.com.

Once done, I will reply to your message proposing a date for our session.

LET'S GET INTO THE SITUATION...

CHAPTER 1

TO START WITH

1. LET'S GET INTO THE SITUATION...

Introduction to the world of cryptocurrencies and CBDCs

Welcome! I understand that after reading the synopsis you are eager to know what CBDCs are and why they could revolutionize the financial system, you are in the right place. But let's stop for a moment. Before we dive into the wonderful world of CBDCs, let's take a little trip into the world of cryptocurrencies to understand it all a little better...

Let's use an analogy: imagine cryptocurrencies as digital currencies, but with superpowers: they are protected by the armor of cryptography and carried by the winged horse of the blockchain. Unlike the currencies you have in your pocket, backed by governments, cryptocurrencies are not controlled by any central authority, and that has good points and not so good points.

In 2009, Bitcoin, the first cryptocurrency, was born, and thanks to its great success, thousands of other digital currencies appeared, each one dancing to its own music, with different characteristics and different purposes. All, however, have one thing in common: blockchain technology and cryptography. Think of the blockchain as a magic ledger that stores every story (transaction) securely and transparently.

And how do you ensure that these stories are not corrupted?

Well, there is a community of gatekeepers (nodes) that monitor and control the security and integrity of the network, so the larger the blockchain (the more nodes), the more secure it is.

In this sense, to define it a little more technically, the blockchain is a distributed ledger technology (DLT) that allows the recording of transactions in a secure, transparent and decentralized way. In a blockchain network, all transactions are recorded in blocks that are linked together chronologically and permanently, ensuring that the information is immutable and incorruptible.

Quickly, its main features are:

Decentralization: They are maintained and verified by a decentralized network of users...

Security: Thanks to cryptography, transactions cannot be modified.

Shortage: Most cryptocurrencies have stipulated limits on their supply, which makes it easier for the price to tend to rise...

Transparency: Although the transactions are private, the number of cryptocurrencies in circulation is public and their traceability is public.

Speed and low cost: They usually have a much lower cost and a very fast transaction speed.

Anonymity: Transactions are executed with blockchain addresses not linked to the actual entity of the person, it would be like being at a masquerade party, you can know the aliases everyone lists, but not who is who.

Throughout this book, we will go into detail about each of these characteristics, so don't worry!

On the other hand, we can divide cryptocurrencies broadly into three types:

Bitcoin has more than 40% of the dominance of all cryptocurrency market equity. Some use it as a store of value, others for pure speculation and others as an index for the state of the cryptocurrency market, what is clear is that it is the most important cryptocurrency of all. On the other hand, the word altcoins come from the term 'Alternative Coins' and refers to any cryptocurrency that is not Bitcoin.

Finally, stablecoins are cryptocurrencies that are designed to have a more stable price and are usually linked to a fiat currency.

Ahh, and a little spoiler: not all cryptocurrencies work the same way. There are different 'rules of the game' or consensus protocols. From Bitcoin's famous Proof of Work to the exclusive Proof of Authority club.

Just in case you want to know more about it, I'll explain above how they differ:

Proof of Work (PoW): First used by Bitcoin, it is based on solving complex cryptographic problems through mining nodes to verify transactions and add new blocks to its blockchain.

Proof of Stake (PoS): It requires nodes that validate transactions to have a stake in the cryptocurrency in question, i.e. nodes invest and block these cryptocurrencies in order to regulate supply and be able to validate transactions.

Delegated Proof of Stake (DPoS): Like PoS, but with a more hierarchical structure. Token holders can elect delegates to represent them and validate transactions on their behalf, almost like electoral votes...

Proof of Authority (PoA): It grants authority to validate transactions to specific nodes in the network, instead of using computational power or participation.

On the other hand, as you can see in the following page, cryptocurrencies can be put to many more uses than just speculating with them, as most of us have believed at some point:

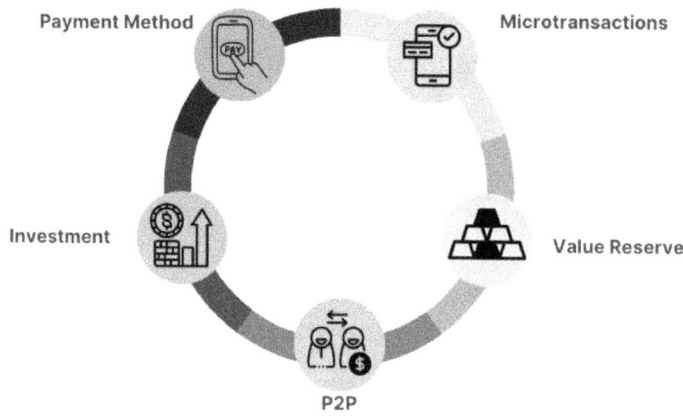

But back to our main topic, CBDCs - what if I told you that they are like cryptocurrencies, but with the backing of the big bosses (governments and central banks)? Both share many similarities; you could say they are cousins! However, the key difference is who is in control.

For central banks, CBDCs are like a diamond in the rough: they see a danger in cryptocurrencies, but also a great opportunity with the technology behind them. And this is where our real adventure begins - read on and let's discover the future of money together!

A financial revolution

Don't worry! I promise that the 'technical' and weirdly named part is over. Here we begin our journey into the world of CBDCs and I assure you, you will understand along the way, why I am so sure how relevant they are going to be in the not-too-distant future and the curious thing is that many seem to be blindfolded to this change. Yes, it amazes me (and perhaps you too, if not now, when you finish the book) how little is known globally about this topic and the impact it will have on the financial dance of the coming years.

So, I decided to play detective! I surveyed John, Mary and everyone who crossed my path. My mission: to make two things clear. First, that the average citizen could use a couple of extra lessons in economics and finance. And second, that many still have no idea what CBDCs are. In fact, with many people to whom I say that I am doing a book and explain that it is about CBDCs, it is very funny to see their faces trying to pretend they don't know if it is a type of diet, a drug or a new type of music!

Let's see the results of the survey....

The first question was very simple:

1. DO YOU THINK YOU ARE FINANCIALLY LITERATE?

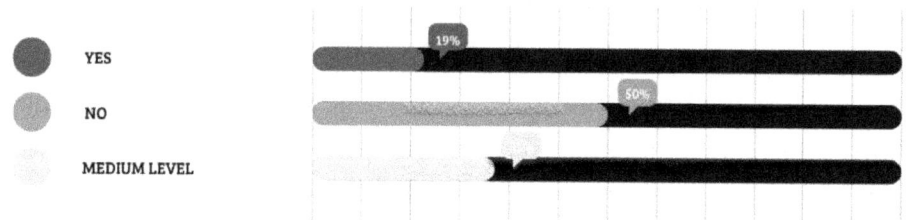

And now for a dose of reality: around half of people consider themselves to have a decent to outstanding financial background. But you know what's even more intriguing? When we stop looking in the mirror and look at the people around us, the answers take an unexpected turn?

If we throw the question towards what we think of the average Spaniard's financial knowledge? Be prepared for some surprises!

2. DO YOU THINK THAT SPANISH CITIZENS, IN GENERAL, HAVE A GOOD LEVEL OF FINANCIAL LITERACY?

And here comes the comical twist: Now it turns out that a large majority of people think that the average Spaniard's financial knowledge.... well, let's just say that it leaves a lot to be desired, i.e. half of these people believe that, in their personal case, their financial knowledge is of a good or at least intermediate level, but at the same time that that of most Spaniards is rather mediocre... How much less interesting!

Although we won't go into the labyrinths of psychology, it is fascinating and, to say the least, curious to see this contradiction...

But to delve deeper into the matter, I posed the million-dollar question to the respondents:

3. DO YOU KNOW WHAT CBDC ARE?

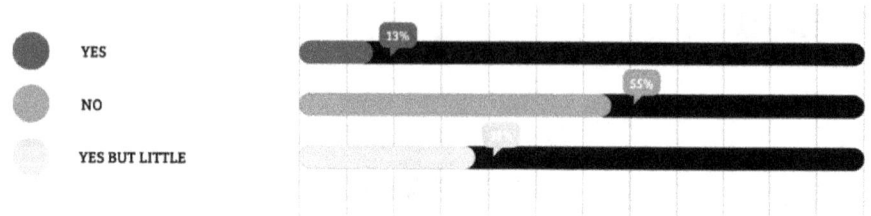

And the numbers speak for themselves: most people are either in the dark about CBDCs or, at best, have a vague idea. The funny thing is that after the survey, I decided to get a little closer and chat with some of the participants. And here comes the surprise: one of them, in the middle of our chat, dropped a little bombshell: he had marked that he knew about CBDCs superficially, but, when confronted with the next question, dive into the cold water! He realized that he really had no idea.

4. DO YOU THINK THEY WILL BE IMPLEMENTED IN THE FUTURE?

The moral of the story: the actual number of people who understand the monumental impact of CBDCs on our global economy... is surprisingly few.

After unravelling the mystery behind CBDCs and asking them about their eventual implementation, bingo! The answers backed up my thesis: once you know what it's all about, people sense that these currencies will play a stellar role in our economy. And to be honest, it is crystal clear to me: CBDCs will be titans on the world economic stage.

This reinforces what I have always believed: we are on the verge of a financial revolution that will transform the economic game board.

And even with all this hype, it seems that many have their sunglasses on in the middle of the night. I bet that, if respondents were to read this book cover to cover, the percentages would skyrocket.

So, before we dive headlong into the heart of the matter, I want to share with you a tool that will be your compass on this journey through the book. Let's dive in!

Definitions to consider

Well, well, well! Before we dive into the fascinating world of CBDC, let's put on our diving goggles. And by diving goggles, I mean a little glossary. Yes, let's clarify those technical terms that sometimes sound like Greek. I'll break them down briefly and simply, so when you come across them in the next few pages, you'll be able to say, 'Ah, I know what he's talking about'. Consider this your quick mini guide, your lifeline, so you don't drown in jargon and can fully enjoy the journey this book proposes. Let's get to work!

Blockchain: Also called blockchain, it is a distributed recording technology used to create an immutable and secure record of transactions. All blocks in the chain, which contain cryptographic information, are connected to each other.

Cryptocurrency: Digital currency based on blockchain technology and cryptography that allows anonymous and secure transactions within the blockchain...

Stablecoin: A type of cryptocurrency that represents a fiat currency with a price equal to that of the currency it represents, issued by a private company.

Central Bank: A financial institution that is responsible for the monetary and financial policy of a country or group of countries. It is responsible for issuing legal tender, setting interest rates, regulating the banking system and maintaining the financial stability of the country or region.

Centralization: It implies that a single entity or person has control and authority over a system.

Decentralization: It involves the distribution of authority and decision-making throughout the network or system, which provides greater security and transparency.

Supply: The quantity of a good or service that is available (on offer) in each market. The less supply there is of something, the scarcer it is and therefore the more valuable it is.

Demand: The quantity of a good or service that is demanded by consumers in each market at a given time. The more demand there is for something, the more people want it and therefore the more value it has.

Token: They are designed to represent physical or virtual assets and are issued and managed on an existing blockchain, not on their own blockchain as cryptocurrencies do.

White Paper: Technical document that describes a cryptocurrency project in detail. It usually contains information such as the project's objectives, the technology used, its consensus protocol, its monetary offer, the team that makes it up, etc.

Smart contracts: A digital contract that is automatically executed on a blockchain without the need for intermediaries. They are used to guarantee the security and confidentiality of certain transactions and contracts.

Trust money (FIAT): Legal tender such as the dollar, euro, pound sterling, etc.

Bull market: Prolonged period of rising prices of financial assets such as equities or cryptocurrencies.

Halving: Bitcoin halving is a scheduled event in the Bitcoin protocol that occurs every 210,000 blocks (approximately every four years) that halves the miners' reward and thus the supply of Bitcoin.

Staking: A form of transaction validation in which users hold a certain amount of cryptocurrency in a wallet to support the network and in return receive rewards in the form of interest in the same cryptocurrency.

Underlying asset: A financial asset or instrument on which a contract or derivative is based and whose underlying price determines the value of the contract.

DLT: Means distributed ledger technology, so the Blockchain is a type of DLT.

KYC: It is a process of verifying that customer information is legitimate to ensure compliance with the regulations governing it.

DeFi: Decentralized Finance is a decentralized financial system built on a blockchain that uses smart contracts to enable a wide range of financial services to be performed without the need for traditional financial institutions.

Perfect! You have armed yourself with a set of essential terms that will allow you to understand not only CBDCs, but also the broader picture of the decentralized economy and cryptocurrencies.

If you feel overwhelmed with all this terminology, don't worry, you don't have to study them. As you go through the book, each of these terms will become clearer and clearer with practical examples and real-life applications. And if you ever get lost, you can always come back here to refresh your memory.

So, with this tool in hand, how about we dive into the world of CBDCs and explore together their relevance, how they work and what they mean for the future of the global economy? Here we go!

GETTING DOWN TO BUSINESS...

CHAPTER 2

WHERE DID THEY COME FROM?

2. GETTING DOWN TO BUSINESS

CBDC, what is that?

It is time to dive into this fascinating world together!

Cryptocurrencies bring with them an incredible capacity for decentralization, an impenetrable amour called blockchain and maintain our privacy thanks to their anonymity. And above all, let's not forget that thanks to scarcity, their long-term value tends to rise!

On the other hand, the CBDC (or 'Central Bank Digital Currency' for those who, like me, like to translate this kind of thing into English) as the evil cousin of these cryptocurrencies. While cryptocurrencies are the big cousin, CBDC is that person who, although wearing a tie, knows how to move in the modern world to win every time no matter who he steps on the road. Issued by a central bank, CBDC is a digital currency backed by the trust and reputation of the issuing institution and accepted as legal tender.

But there's more! Broadly speaking, CBDCs come in two forms: **retail** CBDCs, for you and me, made for everyday use, and **wholesale** CBDCs; think of these as the VIP cards for the big leagues, used mainly among central banks and financial titans. But don't worry!

We'll go into this in more detail a little later.

And just so you get a little gem out of this section, here is a CBDC definition of my own creation that, in my humble opinion, defines them perfectly:

A digital currency issued by a central bank and recognized as legal tender for everyday transactions, and which allows all the advantages of cryptocurrencies and blockchain technology to be used to control people's transactions and improve their efficiency, speed and costs.

Are they all the same?

Being a very new technology and with a short implementation, many types of CBDCs have emerged. To help you understand it better, we are going to classify CBDCs into several categories:

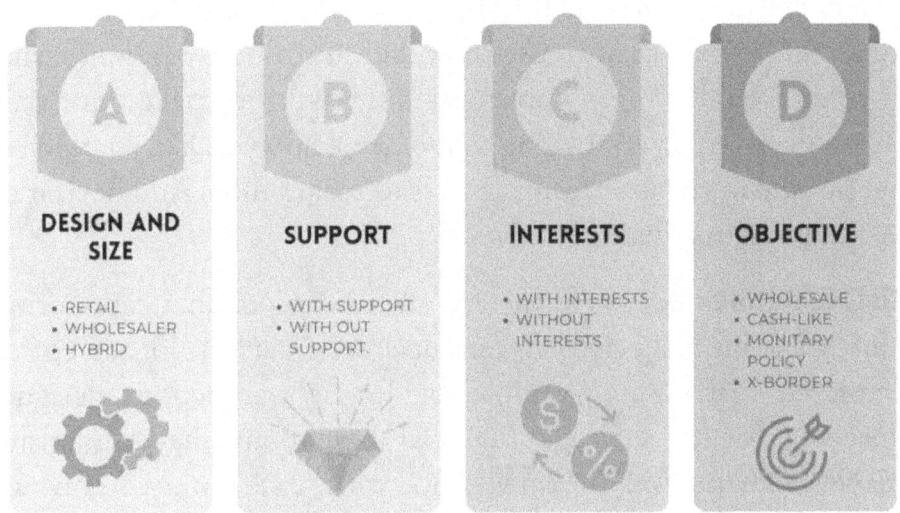

You might be thinking, 'Wow, this is more complicated than I thought!', but don't worry. We're going to break it all down together, step by step, and by the time we're done, you'll be the most cultured of your group of friends.

So, if you're ready, let's start with the first guy!

According to design and size

If we went to an ice cream shop and I asked you what size of ice cream you prefer, you would probably have three options: small, large or medium. Good! CBDCs are not much different in this respect, although, of course, instead of talking about ice cream, we're talking about.... digital money.

CBDC retail: Imagine if we could carry a digital version of the banknotes and coins we usually have in our pockets on our mobile phones and have them accepted as a currency from the very first moment. That's what retail CBDCs are! They are like the euros, dollars or pounds that we use daily, but in their 2.0 version. Issued by central banks, these currencies allow you to make your daily payments, whether it's buying that cappuccino you like so much or that book you've been meaning to read for months. And best of all, no need to carry change!

CBDC wholesale: Now, instead of thinking of that cappuccino, think of a big ship full of cappuccinos. That's a lot of coffee! Wholesale CBDCs are for those 'big league' transactions, designed especially for those huge financial operations that banks and financial institutions normally do with each other. You will probably never use this type of CBDC, but you should know that their existence helps the whole financial system work faster and more efficiently.

CBDC hybrid: Remember that medium sized ice cream I mentioned at the beginning? Well, hybrid CBDCs are something like that. These CBDCs combine the best of both worlds: they are useful for both the ordinary citizen and large financial institutions. They are like that all-terrain vehicle that can be used both in the city and in the mountains. They seek to bring together the advantages of retail and wholesale CBDCs, creating a versatile and efficient digital currency for all through a more complex technology.

According to their support

Think of it as choosing a ticket to a concert. Yes, yes, a ticket! If you get it from an official website, you will have a guarantee that the ticket is reliable, but if you buy it on second-hand platforms, you may not have as much confidence in it. The same goes for CBDCs; the important thing here is what's behind them, i.e. their backing. Let's get down to business!

Have you heard of the **gold standard**? Once upon a time, the money that circulated was tied directly to gold. If a country had X amount of gold, it could only print X amount of money. But since 1971, that system has changed, and money no longer has that direct link to gold.

Today, if you look at the traditional banking system, like the one in Spain, you would be surprised to know that, if we were to suddenly all take our money out of the bank, the bank only has a small fraction in reserve, in fact, the Bank of Spain only obliges them to keep a reserve of 1% of their total deposits.

Which means that 99% of the money we have on deposit in our commercial banks can be used for other more lucrative purposes for them! So, what would happen if we all went to the banks for our money? I think you know the answer...

It's like you have a piggy bank, but only a small percentage of it is actually yours, and the rest is used by the bank to do its own operations. But don't worry, you are covered by the Bank of Spain up to €100,000. The problem would be if we all decided to do the same... What a mess!

With this in mind, let's dive into the backing of CBDCs:

CBDC asset-backed: Remember the old days of the gold standard? Well, this type of CBDC has a similar relationship, but not necessarily with gold. It could be another asset, like a FIAT currency. These CBDCs are like having a note that says, 'it's worth a chocolate'. The idea is that they are more stable because there is something real behind them. However, like everything in life, there is a downside: If the price of chocolate (or gold, or any other asset) falls, it could affect our CBDC and lose value.

CBDC unsupported: Here, trust does not come from a physical object, but from the central bank itself. That is, you don't have a note that says, 'it's worth a chocolate', but rather a note that says, 'trust me, I'm legit'. It may seem less attractive because by itself it has no intrinsic value, but it also has its advantages: it is faster and cheaper.

And that, dear reader, is how endorsement affects CBDCs.

Depending on the interests

Let's talk about something we all love: earning a little more! When you put money in the bank, wouldn't it be great if it grew just by being there? Well, CBDCs offer two different scenarios in this regard, and I'm going to tell you about them!

CBDC with interest: Digital currencies that allow you to earn a return for storing them, similar to staking with PoS cryptocurrencies.

CBDC interest-free: These are like that mattress that many people used to keep money in at home. Yes, your money is safe, but it's not doing 'magic' to grow. It's just like the money we use every day: you spend it, you save it, but you don't expect it to multiply on its own.

Both options have their advantages, but it seems that most of today's CBDCs prefer the 'cushion' rather than those that can generate extra money...

Depending on the objective or problem they wish to solve

Dear reader, tell me something, have you ever wondered why there are different tools or gadgets in a toolbox? We don't use a hammer to screw, do we? Similarly, CBDCs are born with different objectives in mind to address specific deficiencies in our current financial system.

Let's take a look:

CBDC TYPE	ACCESSIBILITY	IDENTITY	INTERESTS
CBDC wholesale	🔒 Restricted	Identified	→ Interest-free
CBDC cash-like	🔓 Universal	Anonymous	→ Interest-free
Monetary policy tool	🔓 Universal	Anonymous	📊 With interest
CBDC x-border	🔓 Universal	Identified	→ Interest-free

CBDC wholesale: Imagine an exclusive club where only certain entities, such as banks and financial institutions, can enter. These CBDCs seek to improve wholesale payment systems and are like that VIP club: only for select members. They are not anonymous (everyone in the club knows each other) and they do not give you interest because their payment systems are based on accounts with a fixed nominal value.

But what if I tell you that these transactions can be accompanied by accounts that DO earn interest at the central bank? Interesting right!

CBDC cash-like: Imagine being able to carry your money digitally on your smartphone. These CBDCs are the bridge between cash and the digital world. Although you need approval to use them, they are ALMOST anonymous (and we'll see why I say that) and they don't earn you interest. And here's the spicy reason: they are intended to replace cash as a more efficient means of payment, to be less anonymous than cash, to avoid counterfeiting and fraud and, above all, because they allow governments and central banks much greater control over transactions.

New monetary policy tool: Imagine a financial superhero coming to improve monetary policy instruments. These CBDCs are universal, almost like the Superman of currencies. They are anonymous and, mind you, they can give you returns. The aim is to harness the power of digital money to play with interest rates, either for or against, to improve monetary policy instruments and thus avoid financial problems such as the zero lower bound or financial crises.

CBDC x-border: These, on the other hand, are like a lifeline for banks in times of crisis. Their mission is to reduce (or dream of eliminating) banking crises. They are open to all, but hey, no hiding places here; they are not anonymous. And don't expect interest. But there is a version 2.0 that aims primarily to address banking crises through a specific currency, issued by multiple central banks to facilitate international transfers. Oh, and they are backed by a basket of collateral. That sounds safe, doesn't it? We'll have to see...

And here's the scoop: although there are many types of CBDCs, the most popular right now are **cash-like CBDCs**. It seems that the dream of many central banks is to say 'so long' to traditional cash, do you think it will happen?

What are its main characteristics?

You know what cryptocurrencies are: those digital currencies we've all heard about. Now combine them with the trust and backing of your central bank. Sounds interesting, doesn't it? CBDCs are something like that. Not only does this make them as legal as the banknotes you keep in your wallet, but it also positions them as powerful tools for governments to implement more fine-tuned monetary policies. So yes, it's like having the best of both worlds, or maybe not... You'll come to your own conclusion at the end of our journey. Let's take a quick look at its characteristics:

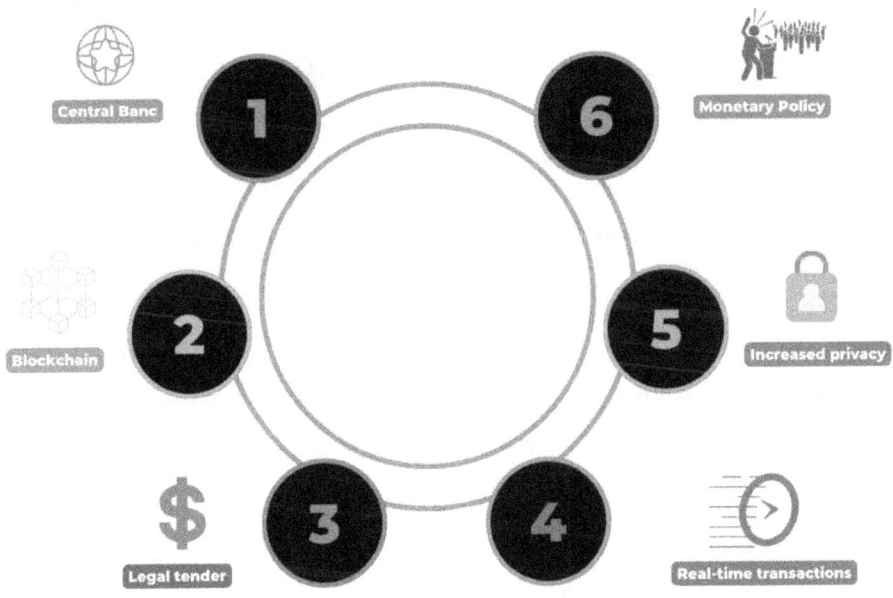

Issued by a central bank: They are issued, backed and controlled by a central bank that decides at all times which monetary policy to use at any given moment.

Blockchain: To ensure transparency and security in transactions, they operate under a distributed accounting technology infrastructure, the blockchain.

Legal tender: They are an official form of payment, which means that they have the same status as cash and must be accepted as a method of payment by all citizens.

Real-time transactions: They can be transferred immediately and with the same speed and efficiency as cryptocurrencies.

Increased privacy: Unlike bank credit card transactions that leave a trail of data in the hands of third parties, CBDCs offer greater privacy.

Monetary policies: It allows central banks to implement more effective monetary policies in case of crises or negative economic cycles.

OK, dear reader, this all sounds very good, doesn't it?

Yes, it does, but here you could differentiate theory from practice or, to put it another way, expectation from reality. To simplify it, let's make an analogy that I think makes it much easier to understand!

OK, think of CBDCs as a futuristic car touted with multiple advanced features as we have already seen. At first, they tell you that this car has autopilot, is super-fast, and allows you to be invisible in traffic. Sounds great, doesn't it?

Free Access vs VIP Access: Imagine that this futuristic car can only be driven by a select few. In theory, everyone should be able to sit behind the wheel, but in reality, only those who have a VIP membership (granted by certain 'garages' or banks) can do so. It is the same with CBDCs, they do not have free access unlike traditional money, in fact, today, in most CBDC projects, the central banks decide who is given access to them and who is not.

Controlled invisibility: The car is supposed to make you invisible on the road, but there is a catch. You have to ask permission every time you want to use the feature and register. It's like being given an invisibility cloak, but always with a sticker that says, 'I'm invisible... but with permission'! Well, it's the same with CBDCs and privacy. So, I ask you dear reader, if you have to ask for permission to have privacy, do you really have privacy?

Travel Log: Even though you can go wherever you want with your car, there is always a drone following you, recording your every move. That's what happens with transactions made with CBDCs; although they can be peer-to-peer, everything is recorded on the Blockchain.

The 'control center' (the banks) knows where you went, how long you were there and how much you spent.

You Cannot 'Store Fuel': While you'd love to store and accumulate your own fuel and watch it multiply (like staking cryptocurrencies), this futuristic car doesn't allow it. But, like any good vehicle of the future, it has the flexibility to incorporate it if circumstances change, as long as the dealer is interested, as is the case with CBDCs and central banks.

To conclude, although CBDCs are presented to us as a financial revolution with many promises, as with all futuristic cars, it is essential to read the small print. And let's not forget that, behind the wheel, central banks and governments are setting the course!

Where did they come from?

Dear reader, I am explaining to you where we are, but, above all, where we are heading and that is why I think it is very important to know where we are coming from. Right?

Well, let's untangle this tangle. Imagine a world where the central banks, those financial giants, see a new kid entering the neighborhood: Bitcoin and its crypto friends. Like the rebellious teenager it is, Bitcoin shows a way of handling money that challenges the old rules of the game.

Central banks, feeling like old rockers watching young punks, decide they can't be left behind.

The result? CBDCs, the banks' attempt to make their own modern, digital version of money, inspired by cryptocurrencies, but with their own controlling twist. While Bitcoin screams 'Freedom and autonomy for all!', the CBDCs respond 'Let's modernize and control you as much as we can!

Indeed, although Mark Zuckerberg's Libra project was a failure, he saw the potential of a globally stable currency pegged to the major currencies and that led several major central banks, notably the ECB (European Central Bank), to take CBDCs very seriously.

The message was clear: the financial world is changing, and everyone wants a piece of the pie.

In this sense, I have to reveal that there is a general idea that Bitcoin was created to completely displace fiat money, but from my humble point of view, Bitcoin was created more as a currency that complements fiat currencies and allows us to have control of our money at all times, using it also as a store of value, it is simply an alternative for those who want more control over their money.

Thus, the International Monetary Fund (IMF) and central banks started to realize that the current monetary system has certain shortcomings, and that the cryptocurrency market opens a gap between citizens' money and them and, obviously, they don't like that one bit, because they can lose control over money and the economy. In a way, this war to maintain the monopoly of money has led to the birth of CBDCs.

This isn't merely about modernization; central banks aim to regain control over major investors who have been flirting with cryptocurrencies, leaving the old currencies behind. It really is one of the simplest competitive strategies: if you can't compete against your enemy, join him or copy him. In other words, they adopt blockchain technology, attract more digital investors and take advantage of this technology for their own interests (controlling all the transactions you make with CBDCs).

Let's get down to business. Although the history of CBDCs is fairly recent, the Bank for International Settlements says it has been thinking about CBDCs for a while (more than two decades), (what are they going to say...) but the Bank of Spain acknowledges that it all started with Bitcoin.

The first bank to start exploring the idea of issuing its own digital currencies was the Central Bank of Ecuador in 2014, half a decade after the creation of Bitcoin and a year after its first halving. Since then, it seems that all banks have entered a competition to see who can create the best digital version.

As of today, more than 105 countries have CBDC projects, which means that 95% of all central banks in the world are studying or implementing their own CBDC. What do you think? It's becoming clearer and clearer that they are going to be implemented, right? Let's continue!

What are they really for?

You've probably asked yourself, what the hell are they for? I mean, what are we going to use them for in our day-to-day lives and why do you say they are different from today's money? Well, for many things! Although most of these uses are also offered by cryptocurrencies. Let's see...

Retail payments

Pay instantly, whether it's to your friend for that meal he invited you to or at the corner shop and say goodbye to intermediaries who make the process more expensive! In other words, we will be able to use them to pay in any shop or to any of our contacts, just like with today's money.

For example, a citizen could download a digital wallet onto their phone and load their CBDCs onto it. They could then use that wallet to store their money and make P2P (peer-to-peer) payments or at any retailer that accepts CBDCs instantly.

Cross-border payments

Nowadays, sending money to another country is like running a marathon with obstacles. Expensive, slow and complicated. But what if I told you that with CBDCs you can do it like sending a text message, safely and securely? Imagine exchanging your CBDCs for those of another country, with no middlemen and no hassle!

For example, a user could exchange their local CBDC for CBDC from another country without the need for intermediaries, which could reduce costs and waiting times compared to traditional payment methods by a huge amount.

Monetary policy

Negative interest rates? CBDCs make it possible. Imagine boosting spending when the economy slows down or putting a brake on when inflation is high. That's how versatile it is! It's a perfect tool to move the economy as you please.

Direct Money: Economic crisis? Thanks to the blockchain, state aid could arrive in the blink of an eye, but this same technology also allows that, in times of crisis, the government has the possibility of forcing you to spend money from your wallet to stimulate the economy through consumption, in the end, it is programmable money, it can be created with a click and 'burned' with another.

Privacy in daily payments

With CBDCs, transactions are like sending secret messages: no intermediaries, more private. But be careful with KYC, if central banks force us to register with KYC as with the e-yuan in China, that message will carry your name and all your data, just as it does now with banks, and that privacy will really become total control by central banks over what you do with your money.

Financial inclusion

CBDCs could be that open door to a more accessible and affordable financial world by offering an alternative to those who do not have access to traditional financial instruments. In fact, according to the World Bank, 1.7 billion people do not have access to these instruments and with CBDCs these users would not need to have a bank account to access certain financial services.

There is a certain rumor that makes sense around this issue, it is stipulated that CBDCs, especially at the beginning, will offer financial services at a lower cost (which makes sense if they want to incentivize users to move their capital to these types of currencies), but that, once implemented, they will have all the power to raise the costs as much as they want.

Also, as you might have thought, it might help some people, but it will obviously deprive people with technological difficulties or lack of money or knowledge, mostly due to age, of these financial services, as they need certain technological skills that many people lack.

Fraud prevention

I'm sure it's the one you've hated the most, because with CBDCs, tracking money digitally is easier than ever. With CBDC, every transaction leaves a traceable footprint, making tax fraud a mission impossible!

For example, it would be much easier to monitor private-to-private transactions for tax fraud purposes as all transactions would be recorded and could be much more easily traced by the tax authorities.

That's why I say it's dangerous, not only can they follow the transactions of people who commit crimes, they can follow the transactions of everyone who uses CBDC with the excuse that some of us might do fraud of some kind! This reminds me of the famous Siri, many do not believe it, but it is obvious that the iPhone listens to you ALL THE TIME, for Siri to activate when you say 'Hey Siri' the iPhone has to be analyzing every word that comes out of your mouth so that when you say the magic word it appears, well the same with CBDC and the control of all your transactions.

Crisis management

CBDCs may provide central banks with more options to stimulate demand and thus combat demand shocks. This is one of the more dubious uses, as for CBDCs to help manage crises they have to be fully implemented throughout the population in order to have an effect on the overall economy.

To put it more clearly, a central bank could charge negative interest rates on deposits or even put money directly into people's accounts (I see this as less feasible), threatening to remove it if it is not spent within a period of time on certain goods or services with a high economic impact to encourage consumption.

Yes, yes, they could force us to spend our money before it flies out of our wallet, not only the money we are given, but also the money we generate with our own effort!

Settlement of Corporate Bonds

The settlement of corporate bonds or even other types of financial assets is currently a very, very slow and costly process and therefore not very efficient, almost as much as postal letters.

CBDCs could therefore be the express courier of the financial world, if they were used as a settlement asset, counterparty risk would be reduced, and everything would be much more streamlined.

Processing and settlement of taxes

With the traceability of the blockchain, CBDCs could be a taxpayer's best friend. It would allow you to pay your quarterly taxes automatically, hassle-free, and with no middlemen!

Plus, thanks to the transparency of the blockchain, imagine being able to track your taxes and see where every penny goes. Although it sounds utopian, the technology makes it possible, the blockchain makes it possible! All that is missing is the political will, and that is why you and I know that this is something that will not happen.

Online commerce

These types of payments are becoming more and more prevalent in most businesses, and more and more companies are starting to accept payments in cryptocurrencies or alternative forms of payment. But with CBDCs, you can buy on different blockchains without the fear of volatility. And with controls that ensure security and transparency in every transaction.

Securities trading

Currently, financial institutions exchange liquid assets with each other daily in an inefficient and costly market due to the lack of available technology and the separate financial settlement process in most cases. Now, imagine a world where large institutions can exchange assets like pieces in a board game, quickly and seamlessly - CBDC through distributed accounting makes it possible! This is super useful, especially in wholesale debt capital markets and money markets.

Offline Payments

No internet on your mobile, no battery, no problem! CBDCs are not just for online payments. Even though there may be power outages or offline areas, there are solutions such as smart cards to make offline payments even without coverage, internet or with the device switched off.

Contributions to pension and savings plans

As you may know, today's pension plans or savings policies are cumbersome to open, but above all to cash in. CBDCs can solve this by using them for quick settlement contributions, addressing tax regulations automatically and guaranteeing simultaneous transfer of contributions. CBDCs can solve this by using them to make quick settlement contributions, dealing with tax regulations automatically and guaranteeing the simultaneous transfer of contributions. You would have your money as soon as you retire!

Tokenized invoices

Dear reader, this use is one of the ones that has the most potential in my opinion and that is thanks to smart contracts. Delays in the payment of invoices can cause a lack of liquidity for companies around the world, not to mention non-payments, which is why CBDCs (like cryptocurrencies) through smart contracts can tokenize invoices to create assets that can be authenticated, transferred, split or merged.

To make it more understandable, the payment, using a CBDC, is transferred directly to the invoice token, which eliminates counterparty risk (risk of the customer defaulting or being late in payment), once the money is deposited in the smart contract, the invoice becomes a tradable asset that can be paid immediately or that the company can resell, split or merge.

In this sense, companies can sell invoices, authenticated by the payer with a cash discount at CBDC to ensure collection.

In addition, this can be applied to any type of sale and purchase negotiation, for example, we could use CBDCs to buy a flat through a smart contract that would ensure that each and every one of the clauses stipulated in the sale and purchase contract are fulfilled.

Example:

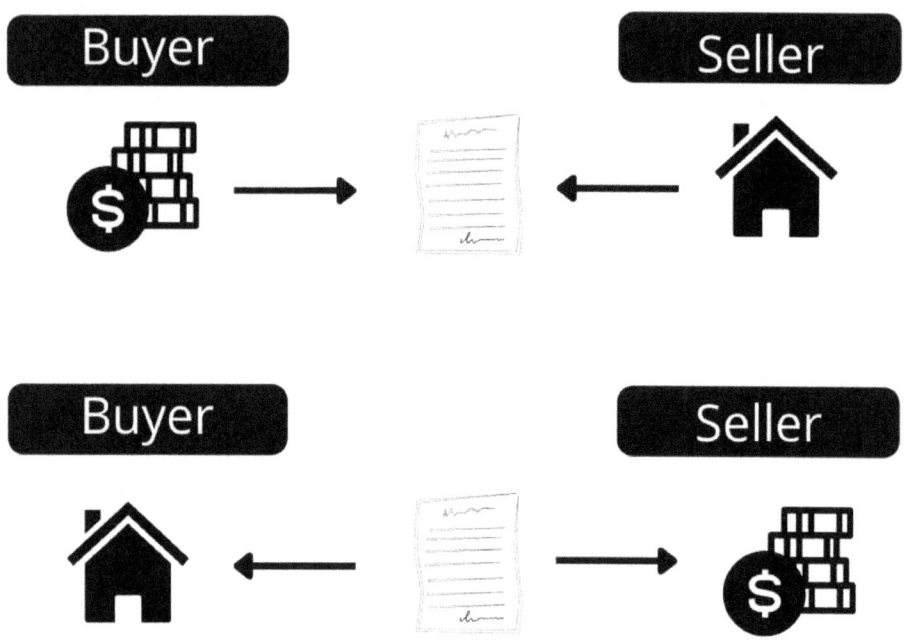

Juan agrees with Pepe to pay 100,000 CBDC monetary units in exchange for the property with cadastral reference x.

Pepe tokens the title deeds of the property and deposits them in the smart contract, which obliges Pepe to transfer the ownership of the property to Juan if he complies with the clauses of the contract.

Subsequently, Juan deposits the 100,000 monetary units of the CBDC in the smart contract and, automatically, Juan receives the property, and Pepe receives the price without the need for intermediaries and, therefore, in a much more agile and much less costly way.

These are just some of the use cases that come to mind and that I think are the most important, I'm sure I'm missing some!

LET'S GO DEEPER...

CHAPTER 3

WHERE ARE WE GOING?

3. LET'S GO DEEPER...

What about business?

As with any innovation, CBDC will also bring opportunities that only the quickest will be able to take advantage of in the private sector.

In this aspect, among the many opportunities that the implementation of CBDC can generate for the private sector, the most important, or at least the most logical in my view, are the following:

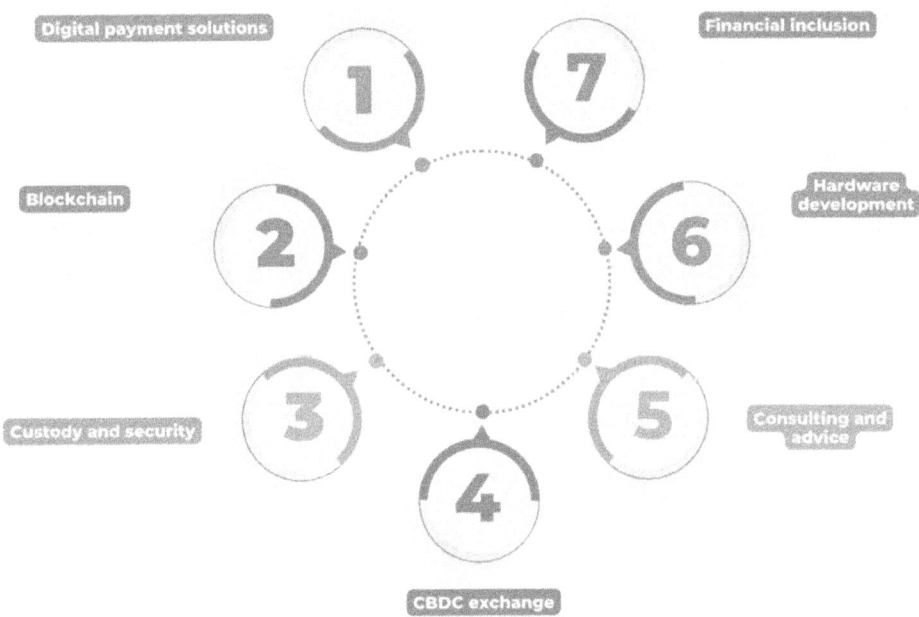

Digital payment solutions: As CBDCs consolidate, interest in digital payment solutions will grow. Companies already established in the digital market, such as PayPal or Stripe, have a great opportunity ahead of them.

But, in addition, giants such as VISA and American Express could also be players in this digital race.

Blockchain: The issuance of a CBDC will unequivocally mean that companies specializing in the development of blockchain technology and offering related solutions, such as data storage and processing, process automation or asset tokenization, will have incredible market opportunities.

In fact, this could represent a gold mine for companies and startups specializing in this technology. Whether it is developed in-house or in cooperation with public entities, the blockchain world has a lot to offer.

Custody and security services: CBDCs will be a very valuable asset, so securing them will be essential. Companies specializing in cybersecurity, digital asset safekeeping and wallets will also have their moment in the sun.

CBDC exchange platforms: Like Forex in traditional currencies, platforms dedicated to the exchange of CBDC from different countries will emerge. A new form of Forex, but with a focus on the digital universe.

Consultancy and advice: Implementing CBDC is a challenging journey. Consulting firms offering expertise in regulations, policies and strategies related to CBDC will be in high demand.

Hardware development: Not everything will be intangible. CBDCs will require physical devices that enable their use in everyday life, especially for offline transactions. There is a golden opportunity here for hardware development companies.

Financial inclusion: As I have discussed previously, CBDCs have the potential to be a vehicle for financial inclusion for those who are currently marginalized from the traditional financial system.

This represents an opportunity for companies that provide solutions such as microcredit, neobanks and other services for disadvantaged populations.

In conclusion, CBDCs are not simply a government innovation. They represent a vast ocean of opportunity for the private sector. Those companies that ride this wave from the start could be the leaders of a new financial era.

So, are CBDCs good or bad?

Let's see, dear reader! I'm not going to be the pimp who gives you the answer, my aim is that you come to your own opinion and that (if possible) you let me know what you think. So, let's look at the good and bad parts of CBDC so that you can generate your own opinion on the matter, since my intention is not, far from it, to convince you of anything. Let's go!

ADVANTAGES	VS	DISADVANTAGES
• Cost reduction		• Loss of privacy
• Improvement of the payment system		• Loss of decision-making capacity
• More sustainable money		• Reduced accessibility
• Avoid banking crises		• Centralisation
• Less dependence on banks		• Geographical limitations
• Greater security		• Cyberattacks
• Ease of use		• Regulatory challenges

Advantages

Get comfortable and pay attention! Let's see what the real advantages of CBDCs are.

Cost reduction: With CBDCs you will save headaches and money, since, thanks to disintermediation, CBDCs allow you to reduce costs.

Improving the payment system: Imagine being able to make your payments at 3 a.m., while eating an ice cream in your pyjamas. CBDCs make it possible! Transactions available 24/7, just like cryptocurrencies.

More sustainable money: Goodbye to wasting paper and metal, not to mention the carbon footprint savings by not transporting that money on any roads.

Helping to avoid banking crises: If used correctly, they can greatly reduce banking crises. But they must be used correctly and without infringing on our rights...

Reduced dependence on commercial banks: Although you will not get rid of banks completely, the balance is now shifting more towards central banks, since, by cutting down on intermediaries, we eliminate banking tasks that are currently done by commercial banks. In other words, we shift the dependence from commercial banks to central banks.

Increased security: The magic of cryptocurrency makes CBDCs a strength. But beware! Because they are centralized, they can be a little more delicate than cryptocurrencies, as they rely solely on the security of a single central entity.

Ease of use: If struggling with complicated applications is not your thing, CBDC platforms come to the rescue. Everything is more user-friendly, even allowing you to use multiple accounts on the same application.

Disadvantages

Now that you know all the advantages and think they are and will be great, I'd better explain some of the disadvantages so that you know 'the other side of the coin', never better said.

Loss of privacy: As I have already told you, your privacy could vanish. It's as if every time you spend, someone is taking notes. They will always know how, when, where and in what way you spend your money. A bit creepy!

Loss of citizens' decision-making power: Although it is a very useful tool for the government and central banks to control and eliminate crises, these measures that we have seen that they can take to avoid crises directly affect the ability of citizens to make decisions about the money we have earned. They can limit what we spend, what we earn, or even force us to spend Yes, less crisis, but... at what cost? at what cost?

Reduced accessibility due to learning curve: For many, using CBDCs is like learning a new language, and not everyone has the patience or the skills to do so. Whereas, with the money of a lifetime, well... who needs instructions? who needs instructions?

Centralization: While an advantage for many people, I see it as a disadvantage, since a centralized system will always be more vulnerable than a decentralized one, while allowing a few to set the rules of the system. With everything in the hands of a few, will those hands be fair and equitable? I think not, and history proves me right.

Geographical limitations: The issuance of a CBDC may have geographical limitations, i.e. it may only be accepted by the country issuing it, and although the mBridge project looks like it can solve this, it is currently a significant disadvantage.

Risk of cyber-attacks: While no one can 'hack' a physical banknote, CBDCs are susceptible to digital malefactors. And if it all depends on a central bank... I don't even want to explain the consequences of a single successful cyber-attack.

Regulatory challenges: This, dear reader, we will see later, but there will be a very long period until regulation is fully adapted and perfectly designed and many new regulatory challenges with complex solutions may arise.

And so, ends our walk on the dark side of CBDCs! What do you think, are you on the digital currency team or are you sticking with your old notes?

Where are we going?

It is clear that CBDCs are clearly a growing trend. It's as if suddenly, every country wants to join the 'cool digital money' club. To give you an idea, according to the Atlantic Council's Geoeconomic Centre, more than 110 countries have joined this digital trend! The best part? Together they account for more than 95% of the world's GDP!

With CBDC or in a study phase   Without CBDC

In fact, countries such as Nigeria, Jamaica or the Bahamas have already fully implemented their CBDC, and many other countries have already launched pilot tests.

Moreover, among the G20 countries, 19 are already investigating their own CBDC, and 16 are almost at the starting line with their pilot tests!

Here we find heavyweights such as **South Korea, India, Japan** and **Russia**. And in the **G7** club? Well, the **US** and the **UK** are a bit behind. Although, the Brits have recently made significant strides with their digital pound or 'Britcoin'. We'll get into its secrets later...

If that wasn't enough, the Bank for International Settlements dropped a bombshell in one of its 2022 reports... it turns out that 9 out of 10 central banks are with their hands in the cookie jar, cooking up their own CBDC, driven by the emergence of cryptocurrencies and stablecoins.

And who is leading the race? **China** and its e-yuan! They are using it in more than 20 regions in Mainland China and the numbers are crazy, transactions exceed 100 billion yuan according to the local press! Although, on the other hand, countries like **Sweden**, **Norway**, **Singapore** and **Canada** have their projects in very advanced stages.

The US 'digital dollar', on the other hand, is going at a snail's pace. Despite being the biggest economic power, it has lagged behind in the CBDC race, the only reason it has wanted to enter the field is because it is increasingly facing further de-dollarization, thanks in large part to or because of Bitcoin and the yuan.

Finally, let's look to the future: according to the visionaries at Juniper Research, by 2030 the CBDC market could be worth 213 billion dollars!

But most of this will be for transactions at home, because it seems that cross-border payments will account for only 8%.

And now, dear reader, comes one of my favorite parts, because I'm sure you've asked yourself, 'What CBDCs are there today? Let's get down to business!

Which CBDCs are currently in place?

As we have seen, there are many CBDC projects around the world, so in this section we will analyze the most interesting and advanced projects in the sector.

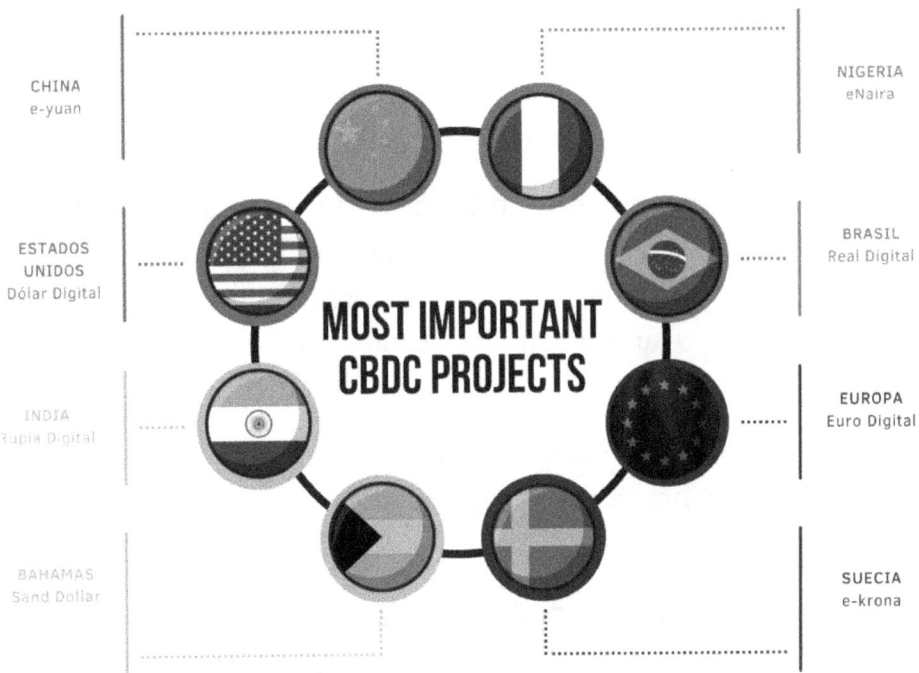

Nigeria (eNaira)
Adoption:

In 2021, while you and I were perhaps learning to bake bread at home (thank you, quarantine), Nigeria was launching the eNaira. But what happens when a country whose population uses so much cash faces a local government-sponsored shortage of banknotes? Exactly! They jump into the wonderful world of digital currencies.

The eNaira appeared just when the central bank had decided to replace the old banknotes with higher denomination ones, at the height of inflation. Bingo! That led more people to try the eNaira, even if not everyone liked it.

In a country like Nigeria where cash accounts for about 90% of domestic transactions, the value of eNaira transactions has increased by 63% to 22 billion naira, according to a Bloomberg report. Also, according to our friend Godwin Emefiele, governor of the Central Bank of Nigeria, eNaira seems to be booming with over 13 million digital wallets, although, this has decreased cash in circulation from 3.2 trillion naira to 1 trillion naira.

But all is not rosy, much of the population seems not to be on board with this new payment system and for now, despite Emefiele's policy efforts, it seems Nigerians do not see eNaira as the best solution, as it is estimated that about 1% of Nigerians have used CBDCs, while over 50% have used cryptocurrencies.

This last figure is revealing, as it clearly shows that, for now, Nigerian citizens prefer cryptocurrencies over CBDCs.

Development:

Now, moving on to the technical details for the geeks in the group: the eNaira is a sort of distant cousin to cash (cash-like). It was created so that you and I, or rather Nigerians, can shop online or physically and send money to whoever is on the other side of the border, so it also has x-border functionalities.

That's the end of the first stop.

Next stop: China.

China (e-yuan)

The e-yuan or e-CNY could perfectly well be called the digital dragon. In fact, it is not a recent invention - no sir! The People's Bank of China (PBOC) has been scheming all this since 2014.

Introduction:

By October 2022, BAM! One-fifth of China's gigantic population, i.e. 23 regions in mainland China, had already adopted e-CNY. Transactions exploded to 100 billion yuan.

23 Regions

Not only that, in Hong Kong, the e-yuan is being used for retail payments at a rate unheard of in world trade.

But China did not stop there. Imagine a digital superhighway where CBDCs from all over the world can seamlessly intersect that's the dream of the mBridge project. According to HSBC's Lewis Sun Lei, it's more than a dream, it's a reality that promises faster, cheaper and more transparent transactions between different CBDCs for real-time cross-border payments.

On the other hand, we all know that the gravitational pull of the dollar is palpable, due to its influence on the global economy and trade relations. But China, with its e-CNY, has a clear mission: to reduce its dependence on the dollar and strengthen the digital yuan.

Finally, according to global consultancy Oliver Wyman, the use of e-CNY in trade between Singapore and China could generate estimated savings of between 11.4 billion and 17.4 billion dollars. This represents between 3 and 5 percent of Singapore's GDP!

Features:

The adoption rate of the Chinese population has steadily increased, and more and more users are seeing real-life benefits. But why has this digital dragon been so successful? For several reasons:

Chinese culture: Chinese society is always one step ahead when it comes to technology. The adoption of digital technologies has been implemented for many years among most of the population.

In addition, Chinese culture values stability and security and the Chinese government has emphasized these values in promoting e-CNY. In addition to these aspects, Chinese society has a high level of trust in its government and its policies.

Use cases: The People's Bank of China has given them reasons to love e-CNY:

- They unify all bank accounts in a single application.
- They can pay via QR code, something already used by millions of Chinese citizens.
- Allow offline payments and 0% phone battery life.

Privacy: Here's the interesting part. China has adopted an approach known as 'controlled anonymity'. Transactions are private, for ALMOST everyone, the BPC can see what is going on behind the digital curtains. It can track the movements of the DC/EP and thus knows the corresponding relationship between the addresses and the identity of the user through a KYC process. In short, your information is anonymous to everyone but the BPC, for which the information is completely open and can know absolutely everything about the personal finances of Chinese citizens.

Adoption:

The e-CNY is like a digital superhero for the BPC. It gives them a bird's eye view and control that cash simply cannot offer. Moreover, it is poised to take center stage in retail and cross-border payments, reinforcing China's vision of a 'de-dollarized economy'.

That is why we are talking about a cash-like retail CBDC that also develops x-border functionalities to de-dollarize the Chinese economy through international trade.

And to close with a flourish: the People's Bank of China has raised its sword and proclaimed that the e-CNY will be the only digital currency in its realm, so the e-yuan will not only be its CBDC, but also the only digital currency in the country.

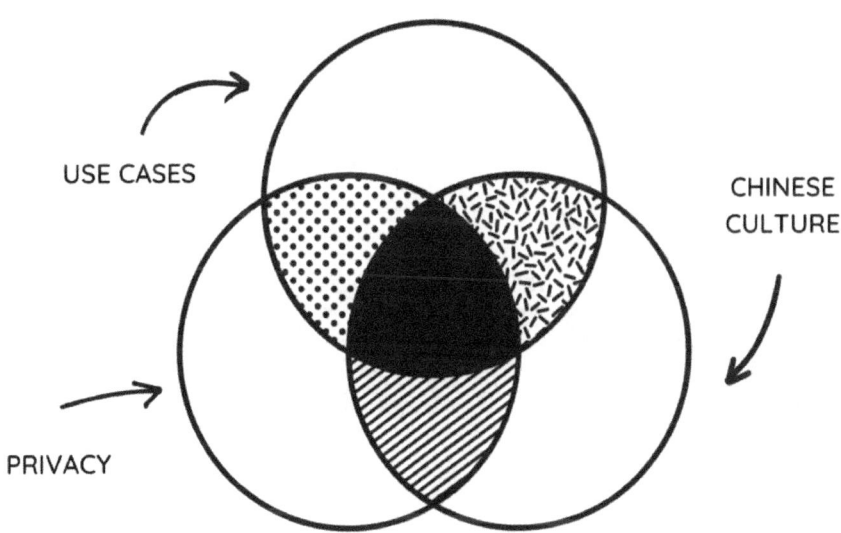

That's the end of our visit to the digital dragon!

Next stop: European Union

European Union (Digital Euro)

It has not yet been implemented, but have you heard about the digital Euro? Well, although it may not seem like it, it is just around the corner! According to Pablo Gil (an expert on the subject with whom I have had the pleasure of discussing the issue) the current pilot phase was scheduled to end in October 2023, and they've done it, they're already in the preparation phase, where the regulation, platform and infrastructure will be developed and if everything goes according to plan, by 2026 we could already have this new type of euro in our 'hands' (or, rather, on our devices), at the very latest!

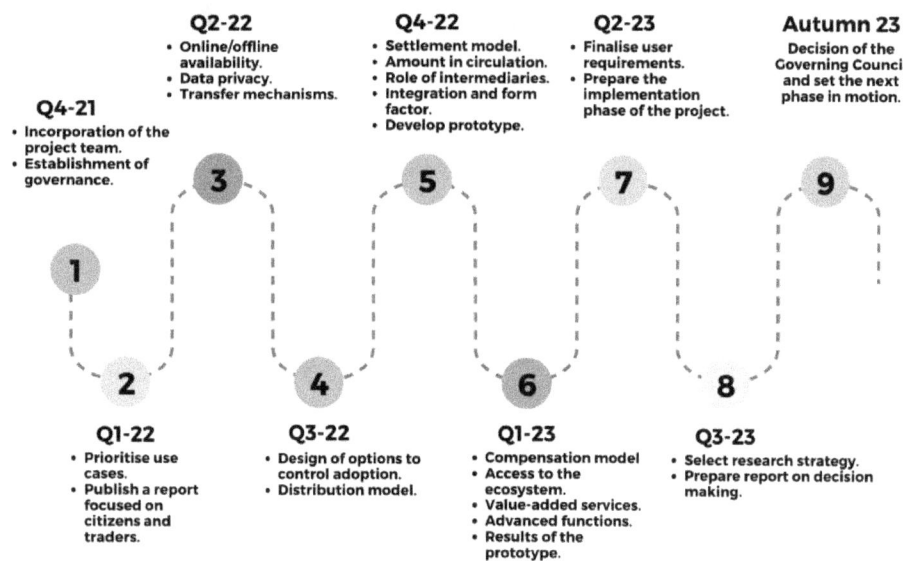

Where do we stand?
Provisional calendar subject to change

Q4-21
- Incorporation of the project team.
- Establishment of governance.

Q1-22
- Prioritise use cases.
- Publish a report focused on citizens and traders.

Q2-22
- Online/offline availability.
- Data privacy.
- Transfer mechanisms.

Q3-22
- Design of options to control adoption.
- Distribution model.

Q4-22
- Settlement model.
- Amount in circulation.
- Role of intermediaries.
- Integration and form factor.
- Develop prototype.

Q1-23
- Compensation model
- Access to the ecosystem.
- Value-added services.
- Advanced functions.
- Results of the prototype.

Q2-23
- Finalise user requirements.
- Prepare the implementation phase of the project.

Q3-23
- Select research strategy.
- Prepare report on decision making.

Autumn 23
Decision of the Governing Council and set the next phase in motion.

Goals:

You may have asked yourself, what on earth do we need a digital euro for? Well, if you check the website of the European Central Bank (hereafter ECB for short), the digital euro will be a secure and easy-to-use digital currency for any citizen of the euro area. But don't we already have a secure and easy-to-use euro? The ECB sets out several objectives:

Goodbye, cash! Although they will not disappear completely, it is a fact that the world is going digital and that is their argument, that there is less and less demand for cash, but I imagine you know that cash is much more difficult to control and investigate, so this CBDC would be another tool (like the limitation on the amount of cash payments), perhaps the most effective, to end up completely eliminating cash. Many ECB members, such as Fabio Panetta, a member of the Executive Board, argue that the idea is to complement cash, not to eliminate it, but the aim is also that CBDCs will increasingly be used instead of cash, which unequivocally leads to the disappearance of cash.

Staying competitive: They don't want to be left behind by other currencies, that's just the way it is. Lagarde herself (President of the ECB) has said it more than once, in the absence of the digital euro, the emergence of other CBDCs (or cryptocurrencies) in large economies could undermine the international role of the euro and take away its power as a currency for international transactions.

For everyone! They argue that they want more people, including those outside the banking system, to be able to benefit from financial services.

OK, but what will this digital euro look like?

It will be a complement to cash, not a replacement, or at least at first, this is a phrase that is repeated in most projects, in others, they directly tell the truth, that the objective is to replace cash, in the end, the objective among these projects does not change, what changes is the way it is communicated or hidden.

You will have privacy, but with an eye on preventing illegal activities. So, let them explain to us how you can have a lot of privacy but at the same time they can see and investigate all our transactions in case we commit a crime?

It will allow citizens to stipulate spending limits to protect us from financial crises or other restrictions, i.e. you won't be able to spend your money as you please.

Usable throughout Europe and, hopefully, in other parts of the world.

There is talk of incorporating smart contracts, among other things! We'll see how it turns out...

It is a Euro. So yes, it will be legal tender like the one we already know.

They want to make it interoperable with other CBDCs to strengthen international relations.

Is it risky?

Obviously, the digital euro entails many risks, do you want to know the most relevant ones? Let's dive in!

Firstly, it would be a misuse of **personal information** and a **lack of privacy** in financial payments. In fact, a video of Lagarde, President of the European Central Bank, has gone viral in which, among other things, she admits that there will be control over the population in a 'limited' way, that it is possible that measures will be adapted in which there will be no control for operations of less than 300€ or 400€ but that it could be dangerous for the fight against terrorism and money laundering and that she does not want to depend on a currency from unfriendly countries or even a currency issued by a private company such as Meta or Google. In other words, they sell it to you a bit like 'We want you to be safe! But it is also vital to prevent unlawful acts.' But the reality seems to be different, i.e. preventing unlawful acts is obviously one goal, but not the only one...

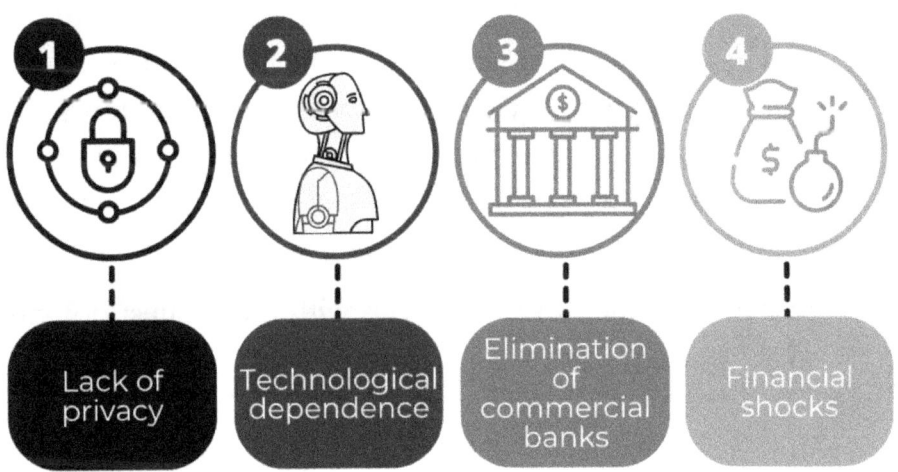

Second, reliance on non-European digital currencies could create **systemic risks** and even jeopardize monetary and digital sovereignty.

Would you trust a currency created by companies outside Europe? It could be dangerous for Europe!

Thirdly, this digital euro could be a game changer for **traditional banks**, as it could create a risk of disintermediation of commercial banking, and although Panetta clarifies that this is not the ECB's intention, it is very likely, since, as we have seen above, one of the main objectives of CBDCs is to eliminate bank intermediation to reduce costs and speed up transactions. What will happen to commercial banking?

Fourth and finally, as you know, investors are always looking for opportunities, and one must be careful about sudden capital movements, as the digital euro would be a very liquid asset and could lead to disproportionate use by foreign investors in times of international financial shocks.

In short... There are still many decisions to be made and avenues to be explored. But what is clear is that in the long term, this complementarity with cash will be a problem, as Lagarde has already anticipated, and it is hard to believe that this is really going to be the case.

Let us now turn to one of the countries with the greatest potential on the world stage, India!

India (Digital Rupee)

Adoption:

In the cradle of civilization, where elephants roam and temples touch the sky, the next page in the history of money is being written! I am talking about the **Digital Rupee**.

The Digital Rupee is a CBDC issued and regulated by the Reserve Bank of India, hereafter RBI. This pilot test is well underway and is already being used as a form of payment in different shops in the Asian country, in fact, in more than 5,000 shops across the country.

In a country where people are turning to cryptocurrencies, the RBI wants to offer a secure and regulated option. Moreover, India already has some experience with this, thanks to the Unified Payments Interface, where people pay with QR codes from their bank accounts, plus there was already a widespread cashless movement.

Interestingly, although India has been reluctant to embrace cryptocurrencies, in May 2023 it teamed up with the United Arab Emirates to study how their digital currencies can work together to reduce cross-border transaction costs and strengthen economic ties between the two countries.

Finally, the RBI is exploring how the digital rupee could work offline to further facilitate payments and is providing a great opportunity for the private sector and Fintech to contribute to these developments.

Development:

Looking further in, two different pilots have been launched, the wholesale CBDC (CBDC-W) and the retail CBDC (CBDC-R). While wholesale focuses on large bank-to-bank transactions, retail is designed for people like you and me. And according to the 2023 figures, wholesale is winning the race! In fact, according to Nirmala Sitharaman (finance minister) in Parliament, by the end of February 2023, the retail and wholesale digital rupees in circulation were Rs 4 crore and Rs 126 crore respectively.

What do you think? Let's move on to the world's leading power, even if it seems to be asleep...

Next stop: the United States

United States (Digital Dollar)

Did you know that the US is not at the forefront of CBDCs? Yes, it is true. Although pilot tests are underway, they are not as advanced as you might think. Seems odd, doesn't it? There are good reasons.

One of the main reasons is that the US has a super-complex financial system - it's like a jigsaw puzzle with thousands of pieces! Plus, they already have a super advanced digital payment system. Imagine you already use Uber, why would you want a taxi? And don't forget that the dollar is the superstar of global trade - it's the leader of the major leagues! Why change?

Indeed, it accounts for more than three quarters of dollar-denominated international transactions, but also in the constitution of foreign exchange reserves of central banks it is relevant, accounting for more than 60% of reserves and more than two thirds of debt issued. Although, I have to say that this attitude is dangerous, for example, do you remember the great Nokia? It was the best-selling brand in the world in 2006, but today it is not even in the top 10.

Not adapting to the needs of the market and lack of innovation. Saving the distances, it is something that can happen to the great American monster.

On the other hand, more than 85% of stablecoins operate in the US! Although not all of them have their cradle there, they do operate under the starry skies of America. And that gives the US jurisdiction to prosecute and punish them.

According to the Digital Dollar Project, hereafter DDP, (a non-profit organization dedicated to catalyzing digital dollar research and experimentation) the CBDC will be complementary to the existing FIAT currency and its properties will be very similar to those of cash. But here's the tricky part: it has to be transparent and, at the same time, take care of your privacy. How? Well, like the movie, mission impossible.

While the US is not running with urgency, there is one dragon that is: China. With developments like e-CNY, the US is feeling the pressure, and it seems that this sudden willingness to create its own CBDC is a defense strategy. So, if the US does not get its act together and its financial system looks outdated in the face of faster options, it could lose ground.

De-dollarization does not sound so crazy anymore, especially after the mBridge results, as this could be a critical turning point that requires a proactive response from the US.

But what does the Fed say to all this? Jerome Powell, the head of the Fed, says they still don't have a date to launch a CBDC and, in fact, they don't even know if they really need one. Although if they were to get the green light, they could launch it super-fast.

Also, this July came with a surprise! The Federal Reserve launched 'FedNow', a real-time payments system, maybe the prelude to the digital dollar?

Who knows, but some experts believe this could be the prelude to CBDC.

In short... while the world is moving at the speed of light, the US may be taking a slower and more reflective approach. Is this a smart strategy or a risk that could cost them dearly? As my father would say, time will tell...

Next stop: Russia, a controversial country of late to say the least.

Russia (Digital Ruble)

Russia does not want to be left behind in the CBDC race and, under Vladimir Putin, has given the green light to the Digital Ruble. With trials already underway as of August 2023, Russia is preparing for a monetary revolution.

With the approval of the bill, the Central Bank of Russia (CBR) becomes the king of the castle. Not only are they solely in charge of issuing and managing the Digital Ruble, but they also have the exclusive power to provide digital wallets, prohibit joint accounts, deny the generation and accumulation of interest, decide who plays and who does not play in the Digital Ruble world, price transactions and decide when banks can offer services and when they cannot.

The Digital Ruble trial will begin with the participation of 13 banks and their clients, testing the waters of this new system. In addition, 30 companies in 11 different Russian cities are already testing payments - it's getting close!

Although the Kremlin sees the Digital Ruble as an advantage for the population, it seems that the real advantage is for them. With full access to user data and the ability to use it as they wish, it is clear who calls the shots here.

With a solid legal base and Russia's powerful economy behind it, the Digital Ruble promises to be one of the heavyweights in the CBDC world.

Let's do a little samba!

Siguiente destino: Brasil

Brasil (Digital Real)

The Central Bank of Brazil has two proposals: a digital real for the general public (retail) and a more exclusive one for interbank transactions (wholesale). The former will be a consumer-facing cash-like CBDC available to the entire population of Brazil, while the latter will be a digital settlement token with restricted access to interbank transfers and central bank-related transactions.

On 6 March 2023, Brazil lifted the curtain on its pilot project seeking to create a decentralized ecosystem and foster the creation of applications and smart contracts. The idea is to start on the Ethereum Virtual Machine, the technology behind Ethereum (the second most important cryptocurrency in existence), allowing only financial institutions to play in this simulated environment. However, the final currency will not be on the Ethereum network, but on one specially created by the central bank, inspired by Ethereum's features.

The security and privacy of citizens is a top priority for the Central Bank of Brazil. Fabio Araujo, the coordinator of the move, is clear: guaranteeing privacy in a world where the blockchain offers total transparency is one of the great challenges. So, we can say that Fabio does want to make a CBDC that does not infringe on the right of citizens to spend their money as they wish and that he does want to give them the privacy they deserve.

As countries move forward with their own CBDC projects, the differences in approach and design become apparent.

The next country is a wonder of nature, The Bahamas. Let's see what kind of CBDCs we find!

Bahamas (Sand Dollar)

The Bahamas not only fascinates us with its white sandy beaches and crystal-clear waters; it is also a pioneer in the financial world. The Sand Dollar, launched in October 2020, made the archipelago the first country to officially deploy a CBDC in the world.

Imagine paying for a tropical cocktail by scanning a QR code on the beach. That's what the Sand Dollar app offers: making transactions using QR codes, cards or even a unique username.

Despite its innovative launch, the waves have not been entirely in Sand Dollar's favor. While it is being rolled out for tax payments, the transition has been slower than expected. Although 80% of all mobile payment transactions in the country are made with Sand Dollar, the Bahamas is a country where cash is still widely used, dominating over digital payments.

The Bahamas shows us that even in small territories, financial innovation can flourish. However, it is also true that cultural and behavioral change is a global challenge in the transition to digital currencies.

Last stop: Sweden!

Sweden (e-krona)

The Riksbank, the Swedish central bank, is not exactly a newcomer to the world of CBDCs. Its e-krona project has been in full swing since 2017 and is already in its third phase of testing. Without a doubt, Sweden is serious.

Many countries have focused on CBDCs as a means of payment. However, e-krona wants to go further. The intention behind e-krona is to enable people not only to make payments, but also to invest and save. Yes, you read that right: investing and saving!

This is a departure from the mainstream where CBDCs are often seen only as a means of payment.

On the other hand, while many countries flirt with the idea of reducing cash dependency and hide their real intention, Sweden is getting to the point: they want to eliminate it.

And while this may sound radical, it reflects a trend that has been underway in the country for years. In the last decade, cash use has fallen precipitously from 39% to 9%. Given this trend, the Riksbank sees no need to hide its intentions. In fact, other countries are likely to follow suit, albeit less explicitly.

Sweden has always been an innovative country, and the e-krona project proves it. With a population already accustomed to digital payments and a drastic decrease in the use of cash, Sweden is the perfect testing ground for a CBDC that seeks to transform the financial system.

WILL AFFECT US A LOT…

CHAPTER 4

CAN IT HARM US?

4. ARE GOING TO AFFECT US A LOT...

What are they really going to improve?

Now that you know more about CBDCs, let's look at what the real solutions are because you've probably heard central banks claim benefits such as improvements in efficiency and speed of payments, financial inclusion or even boosting the solvency of the financial system, but what do these improvements really mean and why do CBDCs deliver them?

Let's take a look!

PAYMENT EFFICIENCY

- Elimination of intermediaries.
- Issuing and packaging costs.

FINANCIAL INCLUSION

Access to financial services for more people.

MONETARY SOVEREIGNTY

Maintain control of the country's supply and monetary policy.

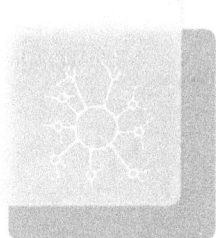

TRACEABILITY

DLT technology makes it possible to optimise the traceability of financial transactions.

Efficiency and cost of payments

Can you imagine making payments faster and at a lower cost? Well, that's what CBDCs could do. Why? For two main reasons:

The key reason here is the **elimination of intermediaries**. Like cryptocurrencies, CBDCs eliminate intermediaries and thus transaction costs. In most CBDC projects, the only participants in transactions or in the holding of money are the central bank, the citizen and, in some cases, a company providing the digital wallet, thus eliminating the intermediation of credit institutions, commercial banks or savings banks, which means a very significant reduction in transaction costs.

On the other hand, despite the fact that, today, digital money already represents 92% and physical money only 8% of the world's money, the aim of central banks is to reduce it as much as possible. For example, if we only consider the dollar, 97% is digital and only 3% is physical. So, if we eliminate cash, we say 'so long' to the **costs of issuance and especially storage**.

Financial inclusion

Have you ever felt excluded from the traditional banking system? If the answer is yes, CBDCs come to the rescue, being a digital wallet for all. With CBDCs, in principle, citizens will not have to have a minimum amount of capital to carry out financial transactions or operations, it will be an infrastructure that will be available to all citizens, it will not have different regulations as currently happens with commercial banking where each bank establishes different rules and costs for its use, and it will also be available to vulnerable groups. But beware, it has its Achilles' heel, as it systematically excludes a significant part of the population.

It is a reality that there is a significant percentage of the population who have difficulty adapting to new technologies and who undoubtedly prefer to use cash as a means of payment because of the ease of use it gives them and because they do not really know how to carry out digital transactions or any other type of online management, either because of their age or their level of education…

Monetary sovereignty

CBDCs can help central banks maintain control over supply and monetary policy in general. This can be especially important in times of economic crisis, when central banks need to take measures to stabilize the economy. In other words, they could use them like a captain at the helm of a ship.

The first of the measures that CBDCs allow central banks to take is to limit the available capital in wallets, i.e. central banks can set minimum or maximum limits on capital holdings or even limit and control the spending of each wallet, force you to spend a minimum amount of money to encourage consumption or even put an expiry date on the CBDC you have in your wallet.

These measures give the central bank a lot of power over citizens and although it may be 'beneficial' for the global economy and for crisis prevention, the reality is that these measures seriously affect the rights you have as a citizen to spend your money as you wish, because that is what you have earned it for…

Despite the above, central banks already decide how much money to 'print' at any given moment and we could say that the decisions they have taken lately are not the best ones in terms of monetary policy. So, while it is a potentially useful tool for crisis prevention, it depends very much on who handles it to be a really useful tool. Do you think they will use it correctly?

Transparency and traceability

CBDCs, like cryptocurrencies, can offer greater transparency and traceability in financial transactions thanks to DLT technology. In this sense, I propose an analogy that I think is ideal to explain the solution it provides; a knife can be used as a tool to feed someone or to murder a person. With transparency and traceability, it is the same, it can be used for good or evil, i.e. CBDCs can allow the central bank to know at all times how much money you have and how you manage it, what transactions you make, to whom, etc. Light, camera, action! With CBDCs, everything is under the spotlight...

This can be used, as the central banks argue, to regulate and control fraud or to control citizens, by this I am not saying they are going to do it, I am saying they can do it and for me that is enough.

If we look at it from the other side of the same coin, although it is not going to end up being done because the central banks are clearly not interested, through DLT technology we could know at all times what our contributions via taxes are being used for, if the state budgets are really being used for what has been stipulated and even reduce (since it is impossible to eliminate it) political corruption. Imagine that! That would be useful, wouldn't it? Well, my friend reader, I am sorry to tell you that, although technology allows it, I don't think it will happen.

Can they harm us economically?

As a good economist, I always like to analyze the economic and financial impacts of any financial revolution, so here we go! How can it affect us economically and financially? Sorry, I'm going to get a bit more technical here...

Well, as you can imagine, giving an answer to this question is complicated, since this impact will affect both the micro and the macro economy, and it is still too early to be able to analyze it. To be able to analyze in depth the impact of CBDCs on the world economy we will have to wait at least a decade, as it will be a slow transition with certain relevant impacts that are not immediate.

But as I like to be adventurous, it is true that certain impacts that the issuance of CBDCs will cause in economic terms are already beginning to be glimpsed, especially in countries that have already implemented them.

It is clear that the issuance of CBDCs will reduce cash, but surprise! it will increase the total money in circulation, which will increase (even more if possible) the country's public debt in order to avoid incurring credit risks.

Moreover, the introduction of a CBDC that provided profits to its holders would cause capital to migrate from other assets to CBDCs, potentially destabilizing the financial system.

For this reason, there are central banks that claim to combat this by capping individuals' holdings of CBDCs as it would help to avoid large deposit outflows, but in my view this solution would risk reducing their usefulness as a means of payment by reducing the scalability and reach of CBDCs.

On the other hand, there is clearly the potential for banks' funding costs to increase if deposits decline while an interest-bearing CBDC becomes widely available. This increase in banks' funding costs, in turn, could have a major impact on the economy at the micro level, as it would increase the cost of credit for households and businesses. Yes, you hear (well you read) right, CBDCs could make borrowing more expensive for you and for businesses!

Moreover, according to a study by the Bank for International Settlements, a CBDC, contrary to popular belief, may weaken the effectiveness of monetary policy, as it could diminish the relationship between monetary policy and interest rates by providing a direct link between the central bank and the population.

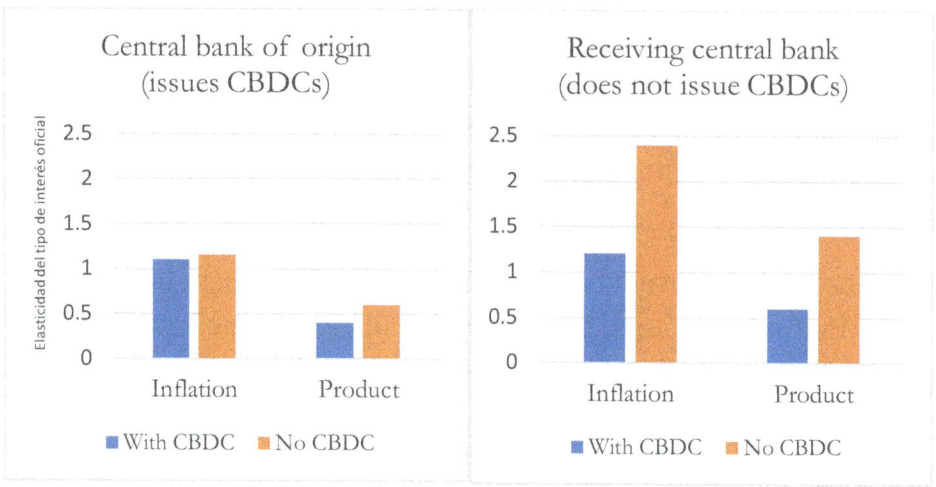

If we imagine a world with globally embedded CBDCs, according to a speech by Fabio Panetta economies without a CBDC may be affected by this, as they will be subject to stronger contagion effects and their central banks would be forced to be more reactive to fluctuations in output and inflation, reducing their autonomy.

The chart shows model simulations by ECB staff that illustrate how the presence of a foreign CBDC affects the reaction function of a host central bank. Such a central bank faces stronger shock contagion effects and may need to be twice as reactive to inflation and output fluctuations.

In contrast, the reaction function of the central bank issuing the CBDC hardly changes.

So, in a world dominated by CBDC, if your country doesn't have one, prepare for a bumpy ride! Economic fluctuations could feel like turbulence.

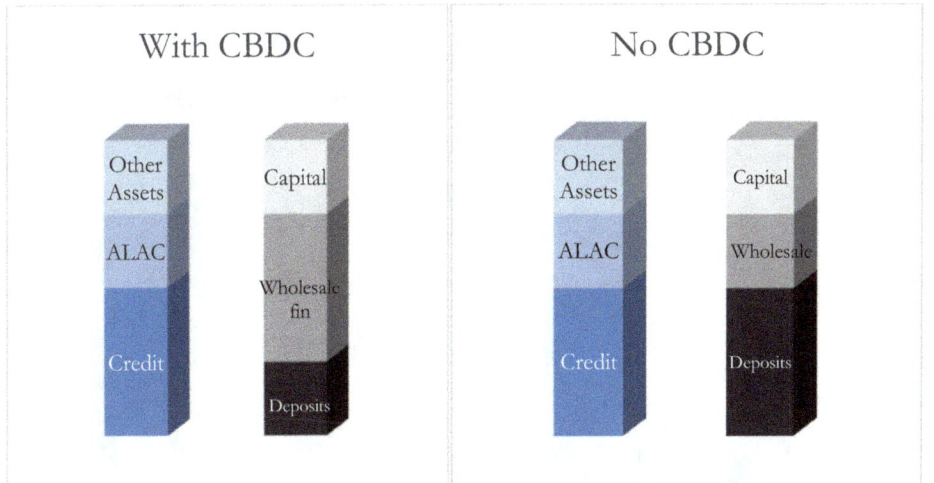

Several major central banks have conducted a joint study within the Bank for International Settlements to analyze the impact of a CBDC. The main estimates are summarized in the chart below. It shows the structure of a basic bank balance sheet without CBDC and with CBDC. The key impact would be the need to shift much of the funding from the retail tranche (deposits) to the wholesale tranche, as a large share of bank accounts would migrate to central bank CBDC.

This change is much more than a simple substitution of funding sources. On the one hand, because it would alter the liability remuneration structure and could raise the cost of funding and squeeze spreads. On the other hand, because it would change the customer relationship and the way in which deposits have been transformed into credit.

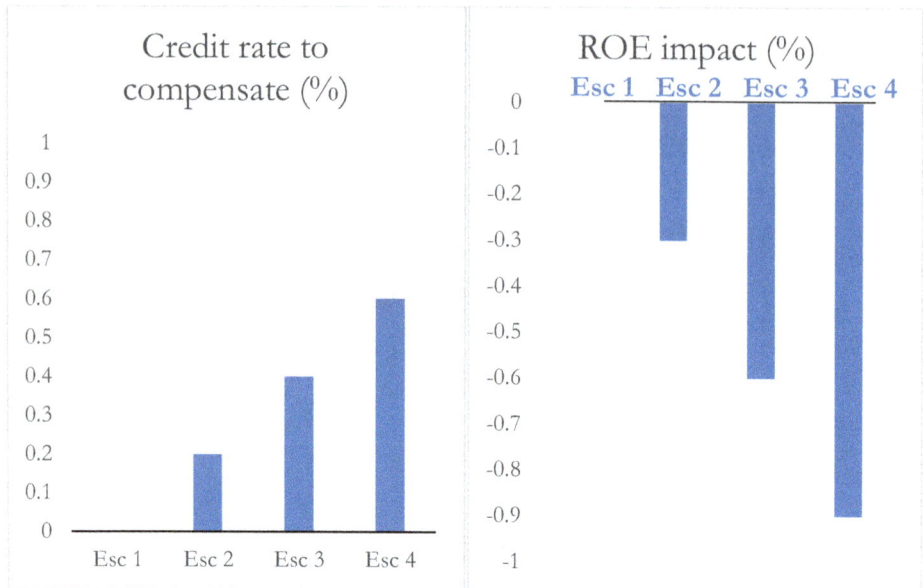

In any case, for a better quantitative understanding, four possible scenarios are considered in the following graph, depending on the percentage of deposits that would be replaced by wholesale funding.

Scenario 1: this transfer would be between 0 and 5%.

Scenario 2: with a switch of between 5 % and 10 %.

Scenario 3: the switch would be between 10 % and 20 %.

Scenario 4: decoupling above 20 %.

Impacts on return on equity (ROE) could be up to 0.9 %. Banks would also have to increase lending to compensate for the impact on their margins. The necessary increase in loan growth rate would be between 0.2 and 0.6 %.

And now, a bombshell to finish! China is already shaking up the financial chessboard. The digital yuan is overshadowing the dollar in global transactions.

In fact, for the first time, the yuan has overtaken the dollar in terms of cross-border payments. The reason? Digital currencies. And although they are still young on the world stage, they are testing the strength of the dollar.

Finally, in China, because of the e-yuan and other digital currencies and innovations, credit card payments are becoming less and less relevant in the economy of the great red dragon.

After knowing all this, isn't it crazy that you know so little about CBDCs? It's time to educate yourself about CBDCs! They are here to stay and will reshape the financial landscape.

What about laws?

But there are not only economic implications, but also regulatory ones, not least because of the difference between the speed at which innovations appear and the pace of regulatory development. We could say that innovation is on an AVE and regulation is on a bicycle!

Our current legal systems may not be ready for the digital tsunami that CBDCs represent. Imagine trying to fit a modern chip into an old radio. Exactly that! Protecting our data and preventing illegal acts are just the tip of the iceberg. In fact, there may be regulatory gaps in addressing risks unique to CBDCs and these regulations may need to evolve as the emergence and adoption of CBDCs requires.

On the other hand, as the **World Economic Forum** reports, the main problem is not technology, it is speed! If policy makers do not speed up, we could lose many benefits of digital currencies or find ourselves with regulations that, well, don't fit!

What is a CBDC? Good question! At present, each country seems to have a different idea. Is it a currency? Is it an asset? Well, currently there is still a lack of global coordination on the classification of CBDCs or stable currencies and without regulatory consistency, a multi-jurisdictional CBDC or stable currency may need to comply with different regulations in each country and legal inconsistencies may arise. What a mess!

As we navigate these uncharted waters, the MiCA regulation proposes a compass. Their idea is simple but brilliant: why not regulate based on risk? So, instead of treating all digital currencies the same, we could have different rules according to their risk potential.

So, it can be risky, can't it?

The enthusiasm for CBDCs is palpable, but there are also opinions and risks that cannot be ignored. Tony Yates, a writer for the Financial Times and former senior adviser to the Bank of England, certainly a voice that cannot go unheard, strongly questions the advent of CBDCs. 'Do we really need them?' he asks. He asserts that money is already digital enough and that the motivations behind CBDCs seem somewhat shady. His experience at the Bank of England gives him some authority, but is he right?

Well only time will tell, the reality is that Yates is also a detractor of cryptocurrencies, as he says (like most cryptocurrency detractors) most of the use of cryptocurrencies is illicit and speculative. But how true is that? Recent data from Chainalysis paints a different picture: only 0.15% of crypto transactions in 2021 were illicit! Do you really think the percentage of cash used for illicit payments is lower?

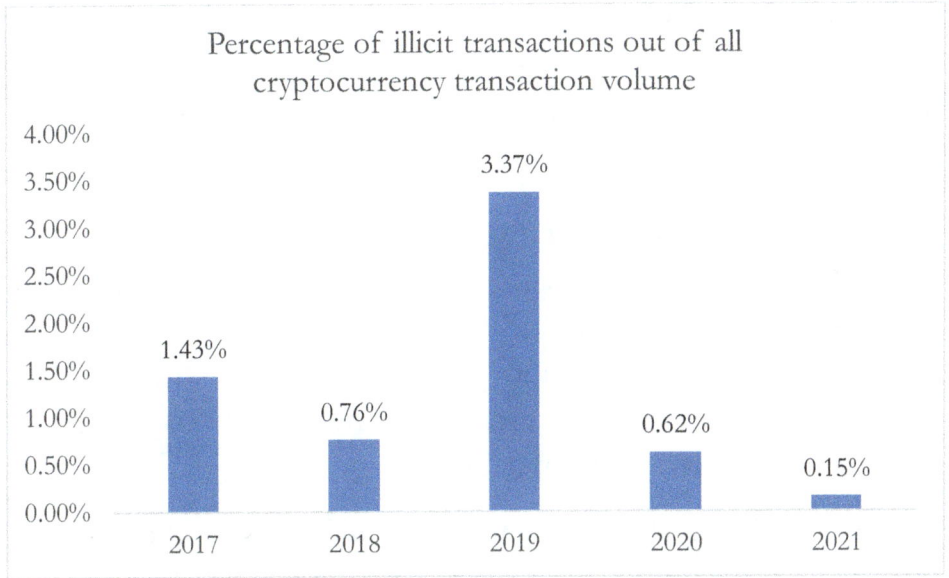

Let's get down to business. Let's break down the most relevant risks.

Financial stability

CBDCs seem to be the golden key to a stable economy, and so they are, provided the hands that wield them are well trained. But, if those hands tremble, we could be staring into the abyss of financial instability. The power of CBDCs is a double-edged sword for the global economy!

Indeed, our aforementioned friend Pablo Gil warns us of the risks. One slip by a central bank and Bam! The global financial system could falter.

In times of crisis, we all look for a safe haven. But with CBDCs, that safe haven could be a digital leap straight to the central bank, and at unprecedented speed.

In situations of systemic financial stress, investors often move their deposits to financial institutions they consider safer or to government securities, and a CBDC should certainly be one.

So, the adoption of CBDCs could trigger a series of changes that could put traditional banks in a bind. From losing a slice of the succulent wholesale payments pie to facing fierce competition from non-banks.

Transmission of international impacts

The issuance of CBDCs for use by non-residents can amplify the cross-border transmission of shocks, increase exchange rate volatility and alter the dynamics of capital flows. In other words, a small event in one country in an economy globally connected by CBDCs can trigger an unstoppable domino effect.

Although CBDCs shine as safe and liquid stars in the financial firmament, they are not meant to be investment assets. As I have explained above, this may expose economies and central banks that do not issue CBDCs to such effects and to further market pressure.

Indeed, according to Panetta, 'significant foreign access to a country's CBDC could result in serious unintended consequences for both the home and foreign countries.

Will CBDCs be the new compass guiding the global economy or the iceberg that sinks it?

Exchange rate volatility

This risk is somewhat related to the previous one: if one country launches a particularly tempting CBDC, investors may flock to it like flies to honey, strengthening the issuing country's currency and leaving other currencies behind, or, in other words, the tempting currency will appreciate relative to the others. What if it is not just one country that launches a tempting CBDC? In a scenario where several central banks enter the scene with their own digital currencies, there could be a lot of competition to attract investors and traders, which could lead to volatility in the exchange rates of the different CBDCs.

Citizen control

This risk, unlike all the others, only affects citizens, it does not affect central banks, indeed, one could say that it affects central banks positively.

As we move into the digital age, we open the door to unprecedented conveniences. But at what price? CBDC has two sides: a bright side of ease and a dark side that watches every step we take.

While paper money has always offered us that cloak of anonymity, centralized digital currency can strip it away. Imagine a world where every transaction, every penny spent, is recorded in a ledger to which the government has direct access.

Integration with social rating systems opens up even greater opportunities for punishment or rewards. A Tweet disagreeing with government policy?

A traffic ticket you forgot to pay? With just a few lines of code, the government could have unprecedented control over your finances. Today, in places like China, population scoring is already a palpable reality.

A rating that not only analyses your financial behavior, but also your opinions and behaviors. Imagine being refused a loan not because of your credit history, but because of your 'social history'. Sound like a movie, right? Well, there are real cases in China where a citizen has been denied a loan because of his credit score because he posted content against some government opinion.

For this reason, if issued at the retail level or by a less benevolent government, it can represent a potentially worrying assault on privacy and consumer protection.

In short, while CBDCs may bring numerous advantages, the issuance of digital currencies at the retail level may call into question a basic right of the citizen, the freedom to manage their money as they see fit.

Dear reader, just a closing thought, what will prevent CBDCs from becoming a weapon against citizens or potentially blocking legitimate transactions by groups that simply have different political ideologies?

The answer is simple, it depends only on the will of central banks, because CBDC technology allows them to do so.

Competition and monopoly

Due to several aspects, there are fewer and fewer commercial banks, CBDCs may be the key factor in further reducing the number of commercial banks, leading to less competition and even to the possibility of monopoly in the financial market in some countries.

But what happens when there is little choice? In the worst-case scenario, we could find ourselves in a market where a single player dominates the financial spectrum.

Lack of competition has historically led to higher costs, less innovation and lower quality of service. For the ordinary user, this could translate, above all, into higher tariffs.

Local currency

If a CBDC were used outside its jurisdiction and widely adopted in a third country, it could supplant the local currency entirely and lead to it losing its function as a means of payment, unit of account and store of value, especially in less developed economies with unstable currencies.

An economy where the local currency, with a history and culture behind it, gradually fades away, replaced by a foreign CBDC would not only be a cultural loss, but could bring instability and vulnerability to the local economy.

The phenomenon of a foreign currency dominating a local economy is not new. The US dollar, with its power and stability, has already played this role in several nations, especially in countries with fragile economies.

CBDCs, in their digital format and with the advantages they offer, could do this on an even larger scale and at a faster pace.

Technological risks

Now let us look at the last major risk. In an era where everything is digital, technological threats have become increasingly sophisticated and CBDCs, as they enter this domain, are not immune to these risks. Although the promises of blockchain technology suggest a high level of security, one cannot ignore the fact that any system, no matter how advanced, has its vulnerabilities.

And most worrying of all, CBDCs will shift significant technological risks to the public sector and ultimately to taxpayers, who will be the most affected by this type of technology!

Moreover, while traditional cryptocurrencies pride themselves on their decentralization, a CBDC is by nature centralized, being under the control and supervision of its central bank. This centralization can become an Achilles' heel, offering a single point of attack.

If a commercial bank experiences a technological failure or is the victim of a cyber-attack, the repercussions are severe but limited to its customers and shareholders.

But when it comes to a central bank, which oversees and ensures the stability of a national economy, the consequences can be catastrophic.

Moreover, just as the failure of any bank undermines the credibility of banking, a CBDC has the potential to transfer that risk to central banks and therefore the risk is much greater.

In the end, it is common sense, a digital currency is just that, digital and as such it can be programmed or hacked, any hack or even technological error by a central bank could paralyze the economy of an entire country. Moreover, you will agree with me that in a war it is easier to attack the enemy if he concentrates all his troops in the same base. That is why it is much more difficult to hack a digital currency like Bitcoin, which is decentralized and has thousands of 'castles'.

Now that we have seen the risks and you are becoming an expert on CBDCs, let's take a look at a real project from the inside. From the inside? Yes, I have been in contact with a member of the CBDC unit of the central bank of this country, so I have fresh information! Let's get down to business!

A real project from the inside - Britcoin What is it?

The Britcoin, also known as the digital pound, emerges as a proposed digital currency issued by the Bank of England and denominated in pounds sterling so that the British population could use it for everyday transactions. Moreover, as highlighted on the Bank of England's official website, the intention is not to replace cash, but to complement it.

How do the Bank of England and HM Treasury define it? In a similar way: 'Electronic version of cash issued by the Bank of England and accessible through digital wallets provided by private companies'.

Among other things, they make it clear that it is NOT going to be created to generate interest nor to save or invest with it. They are very clear, the digital pound is intended for everyday spending, not for saving.

Despite being at a very early stage, in February 2023 after the announcement by the UK Treasury and the Bank of England regarding the digital pound, searches for 'digital currency' in the UK increased fourfold, so it is clear that this type of currency is increasingly in demand among the UK population.

Ben Broadbent, Deputy Governor for Monetary Policy, has more than once emphasized the advantages of the digital pound at Bank of England conferences and it should not be forgotten that London is currently the leading city in terms of cryptographic centers or, in other words, the first Crypto Hub in the world! So, it has very powerful companies in the sector.

On the other hand, although it is not mentioned on the main page, they are also studying the possibility of implementing a wholesale CBDC to improve existing systems, through the efficiency and transparency provided by DLT technologies and the availability to operate 24 hours a day, seven days a week, to encourage and enable innovation in the private sector and to implement a new infrastructure.

In fact, according to Charlie (my plug), a member of the CBDC unit of the Central Bank of England, many technological decisions have not yet been taken and will probably be taken in the next phase, the design phase.

How will it be used?

The Bank of England's idea regarding the use of Britcoin is that every citizen would have their own private account in their own virtual wallet and, they say, the Bank of England would not have access to any of your data nor would they be able to see what your money is spent on, as you would deal directly with your wallet provider and they would have your data to identify you and avoid crime or tax fraud.

But on the other hand, they make it very clear that privacy would continue to be protected by data privacy regulations and would not be shared with either the government or the Bank of England, since, in the end, your wallet provider will have all your data and the basis of the CBDC is a blockchain in which you can know at all times how your money moves, so if the provider gives our identification to the government, they could know at all times where and how our money moves. Are they hiding something from us, dear reader?

In fact, if we read the small print of the Consultation Working Paper prepared by the Bank of England (which I have done), it leaves the door ajar to what I point out, 'companies that have personal data can also share that data as long as there is a legal basis' so, although it would be the wallet providers who would have our data, both the government and the Bank of England could access the data of British citizens and therefore all the financial information they provide.

Moreover, from what I have been told and from what I have been able to investigate, the Bank of England's intention is to eliminate intermediaries as far as possible in transactions with its CBDC (in this case, to eliminate commercial banks as intermediaries), so there would only be the following figures:

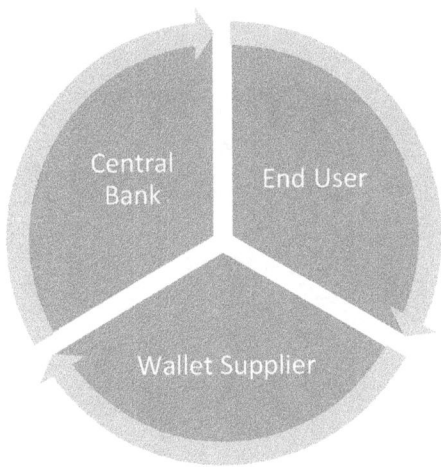

On the other hand, the intention of the Bank of England, while not controlling us, is to set a limit on the number of digital pounds that British citizens could hold. They say this would give them time to understand the impact on the financial system.

Once they have analyzed the impact on the financial system and people's usage, they would 'review' the limit.

During my conversation with Charlie, after asking him about the digital pound cap, he said something to the effect that the limit that will be set is on the number of digital pounds that an individual can own and that this limit may change over time depending on the effects of the digital pound on the financial system. Do you buy it? In a way it makes sense...

Roadmap:

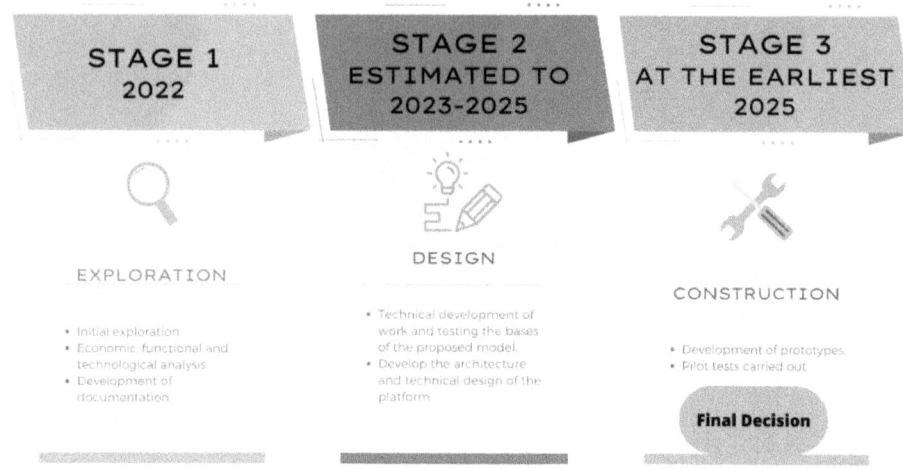

As we can see from the roadmap produced by the Bank of England and HM Treasury, Phase 2, the design of the CBDC, has already been implemented in 2023 and, from what I have been told from the inside, is scheduled to end between 2025 and 2026.

In conclusion, the UK is stepping fully into the digital currency era with its proposed Britcoin. While there are still uncertainties and concerns, especially around privacy and ownership limits, the adoption of CBDCs around the world is a trend that seems inexorable.

Despite being at an early stage, with London as a leader in crypto innovation, it is uniquely positioned to lead this digital financial transformation.

HATEFUL COMPARISONS ...

CHAPTER 5

OUT WITH PREJUDICE PLEASE

5. HATEFUL COMPARISONS...

Are they different from cryptocurrencies?

¿ Ever wondered how CBDCs differ from cryptocurrencies like Bitcoin? Welcome to the club! But don't worry, you're about to find out.

Despite the technological similarities, there is a big difference between the two. Cryptocurrencies like Bitcoin are like the rebels of the financial world: decentralized, and their value depends on supply and demand. CBDCs, on the other hand, are issued by central banks, and backed by the trust we have in those banks.

They are so similar that, even though central banks don't like this classification, CBDCs are considered by many experts as one type of crypto asset and cryptocurrencies as a different type of crypto asset, i.e. they are first cousins!

Shall we dig a little deeper? Let's go! Cryptocurrencies are decentralized digital mediums of exchange that use blockchain technology to ensure the security of transactions, while CBDCs are digital currencies issued by a central bank and are considered a form of legal tender as well as being backed by the trust of the issuing institution. Let's look at the key differences on the next page:

	CBDC	Cryptocurrency
Emitter	Central Bank	Private company or decentralized network
Centralization	Centralized	Decentralized
Value	Backed by a central bank	Depends on supply and demand
Regulation	Legal tender	Most outside the scope of regulation

Emitter: Cryptocurrencies are like a teamwork of a global community. On the other hand, CBDCs have only one boss: the country's central bank.

Centralization: Cryptocurrencies are decentralized, while CBDCs are centralized, meaning that their issuance and control is in the hands of a single entity, in this case the central bank. To use an analogy: cryptocurrencies are like a party without a host, where everyone participates. CBDCs, on the other hand, are like a dinner party with a host who decides the menu.

Value: The value of a cryptocurrency is purely based on market supply and demand, whereas the value of a CBDC is backed by the central bank.

Technology: Both share one thing in common: a fascination with technology! But while cryptocurrencies are loyal to the blockchain, CBDCs can be more flexible with their technology choices, even though most of them use their own blockchain.

Purpose: Cryptocurrencies are mainly used as a means of payment, investment or store of value, while CBDCs are also used as a means of payment, to facilitate financial transactions and to support central bank monetary policy.

Regulation: Cryptocurrencies are often outside the scope of government regulation, while CBDCs are subject to supervision and regulation by central banks and other financial authorities.

Importantly, the implementation of CBDC can be seen as an attempt by central banks to harness the benefits of blockchain technology and the digitization of the economy, while retaining the advantages of centralization and control of monetary policy.

But the truth is that cryptocurrencies have been created as a decentralized alternative to the traditional financial system and are increasingly finding wider use in different contexts.

What about Bitcoin? It is special, and not just because it was the first cryptocurrency. It has three characteristics that no other digital asset that can be considered a store of value or wealth has. BTC has a quantitative limitation of 21 million units, i.e., at most there will be 21,000,000 units of Bitcoin and no more can be created, so it is scarce and finite, you don't have to be a genius to know how that affects the value of an asset.

To explain this there is an analogy that I love. Imagine a desert island where there are a hundred people without food and from a plane we throw them a banana, that banana will have an immense value, but, if minutes later, we send a box with thousands of bananas, the value of the previous banana ends up being insignificant. It is common sense, right? Well, the economy, as difficult as it may seem, works the same way!

In fact, it has a certain relationship with the inflationary crisis of 2022 in which the excessive printing of banknotes by the FED and the European Central Bank has caused a very large loss of purchasing power for the population, which is why I believe that the scarcity of Bitcoin is such a relevant characteristic to consider it a store of value over time.

On the other hand, its technological structure makes it a very secure asset when it comes to making transactions with it, since, once a transaction is made, it is irrevocable and must have been validated by the majority of the nodes in the network.

Finally, approximately every four years the famous 'halving' occurs, which reduces the issuance of Bitcoin by half, so that not only is there a finite number of Bitcoins, but also the issuance of new units is reduced each time, i.e. fewer and fewer Bitcoins are 'manufactured'. This is obviously an important factor in the long-term upward trend in the value of Bitcoin.

So, what is the future? That is the million-dollar question. Come on, I'm going to get involved, although I don't have a crystal ball...

In my opinion, both will coexist and, as Pablo Gil told me in the interview we had, many cryptocurrencies will disappear (which will benefit the cryptocurrency sector) and only those that really provide real value, such as Bitcoin, will survive. In this sense, Bitcoin may even benefit, because much of the capital of these cryptocurrencies that will disappear will go into the Bitcoin blockchain and its value will continue to rise, but, in the end, this is just an opinion.

On the other hand, I'm sure there's a question you've asked yourself too; **How will CBDCs relate to cryptocurrencies? In other words, will we be able to exchange one for the other?**

Well, it is too early to tell, but if we look at economies like China or Nigeria, currently exchanging CBDC for cryptocurrencies is done from an Exchange, i.e. in the same way as traditional currencies. In order to go into a little more depth, I asked Charlie from the Bank of England's CBDC unit this same question and he made it clear that the priority is to make CBDC interoperable with FIAT currencies only, opening the door in the future to interoperability with stablecoins, but in no case with cryptocurrencies such as Bitcoin, since according to him 'they are very similar to shares'. Therefore, in the case of the digital pound and surely in the majority of CBDCs, they can only be exchanged through an exchange, so that the money entering and leaving the system could be tracked at all times thanks to KYC, just as with traditional currencies at present.

Finally, as Pablo Gil reminded me in our interview, it is important to note that the conversion of CBDC to cryptocurrencies might be subject to specific regulations. So dear reader, only time will tell!

Which crypto asset will be the most used, we shall see!

What is the difference with Stablecoins?

At first glance, CBDCs and stablecoins look like twin sisters of the digital world. But if you scratch the surface a bit, you'll see that they have distinct personalities and purposes. Ready to find out what makes them unique? Let's take a look!

Stablecoins are a form of cryptocurrency that function as digital representations of the dollar, the euro and other currencies or assets such as gold. These cryptocurrencies were born for several reasons, but the most important ones were to solve the high volatility of cryptocurrencies.

For a stablecoin to be sound, it must be backed by real money in the same amount as that issued in cryptocurrencies, i.e. Tether (USDT), for example, is the most important stablecoin in the market whose collateral is mostly US government bonds, corporate bonds and actual dollars that validate each USDT unit in circulation.

Like the entire sector, they have been in question for many reasons since their creation, one of the most important of which is regulation, since in certain countries, as has happened with cryptocurrencies, regulators have prohibited the issuance of these.

On the other hand, there have been cases in which some stable currencies, not having sufficient backing or not having been well managed, have fallen into oblivion.

Now that you know what stable currencies are, **let's look at why people confuse them...**

CBDCs and stablecoins are both crypto assets linked or related to a FIAT currency, both have the possibility of unlimited issuance, both need a backing of some kind to be considered solvent and both are created by trusted third parties.

But the reality is that there are many **differences** between the two:

CBDCs are the baby of central banks, while stablecoins usually emerge from private companies or decentralized networks.

CBDCs are legal tender, they are currencies in their own right, so they do not have a physical money backing, they are usually backed by other types of assets such as government debt or simply the trust and credibility of the central bank in question. Stablecoins, on the other hand, must be backed by tangible assets.

Although both use blockchains, stablecoins usually operate on existing networks, while CBDCs create and control their own network.

	CBDC	Stablecoin
Emitter	Central Bank	Private company or decentralized network
Centralization	Centralized	Centralized or decentralized
Support	Backed by a central bank	Backed by FIAT money or other assets
Technology	Blockchain or proprietary DLT	Existing blockchain

The similarity between CBDCs and stable currencies can pose a problem, because if regulators choose to treat retail CBDCs outside the existing legal framework for crypto assets, it is important to ensure that they close any regulatory loopholes to cover the risks of CBDCs. Regulation is key. While both digital currencies can co-exist in the future, it is critical that the rules of the game are clear and fair for both parties. If we favor one over the other, we could unbalance the market.

With the entry of CBDCs, stable currencies may be affected and many of them may disappear, since most of them are backed by physical currency (dollar) in banks and, as it is foreseeable, once CBDCs come out in key countries where stable currencies have some power, they will be the main enemies. In fact, two important decentralized stable currencies have already been attacked, it is not really known by whom, and because of these attacks one was greatly affected (DAI) and the other disappeared (UST).

What makes them different from today's money?

In order to answer the question **'What is the real difference between CBDCs and today's FIAT currencies in digital form?'** alone, there are many different theories, but the reality is that there are some subtle differences between CBDCs and FIAT currencies in digital form that could have major implications for the future of our economy.

CBDCs are issued directly by the central bank, while digital fiat currencies are issued by financial institutions and backed by the government of the issuing country.

CBDCs can be designed to function differently from FIAT currencies, they could be designed to allow transactions directly between individuals and central banks or individuals (P2P) without the need for a financial institution as an intermediary.

Digital FIAT money requires an internet connection, some CBDCs are developing functionalities to operate without it.

While today's digital FIAT money is simply a more convenient way of using physical money, CBDC is a completely new digital currency that is backed by the trust and credibility of the central bank that issues it.

The differentiating factor, without a doubt, is the blockchain or DLT technology with all the benefits that we have already seen that it can provide, above all, in terms of the control that it can allow the central bank to have over the economy and the money supply.

	CBDC	Traditional digital money (FIAT)
Emitter	Central Bank	Financial institutions backed by the government of the issuing country
Offline	Online and offline digital transactions	Online-only digital transactions
Validity	Fully official currency in its own right	More convenient form of traditional money
Technology	Blockchain or proprietary DLT	No DLT technology available

If you are an average citizen, as I am sure you are, the differences in your daily life may seem minimal. You may notice that your transfers are a little faster or that your bank's interface has changed. But apparently, you will not notice big changes, so it is normal to wonder what the difference is between using CBDCs as a means of payment and using a debit/credit card or 'Bizum'.

All these types of operations are carried out by financial institutions using customers' bank accounts. **These operations are not fully supported by the central bank.**

In addition, payments are not necessarily immediate and, in many cases, bear commissions.

With CBDCs, individuals have direct access to their own account at the central bank, without the need for the commercial bank as an intermediary. In addition, there are intrinsic consequences of CBDCs that are not present in today's money, such as the fact that, as programmable money, it can have an expiry date.

PERSONAL OPINION AND REFLECTIONS

CHAPTER 6

WHAT DOES THE AUTHOR MAKE OF ALL THIS?

6. PERSONAL REFLECTIONS

What do I do now?

According to the latest IMF data, 81 central banks, representing 76% of the world's population, have shown interest in implementing CBDCs and, of these, more than two thirds will implement them before the end of the decade, i.e. implementation is inevitable. Therefore, protecting oneself from the risks that such implementation may cause, or at least mitigating them, is extremely complicated, as it is not only a new currency, but much more than that, the implementation of CBDCs means completely changing the financial system we currently have.

As it is, there are people who are against CBDCs and that their method of eliminating the risks of the new financial order is the cryptocurrency ecosystem.

Despite what many people think, mostly out of ignorance, cryptocurrencies are not just a type of digital currency (the name cryptocurrency to me does them a disservice, in my opinion, a more accurate name would be crypto asset), they are much more than that, especially thanks to DeFi which turns them into a whole parallel financial system, In fact, I know people who work in the cryptocurrency sector, who get paid in cryptocurrencies for their work, who pay in establishments that accept cryptocurrencies and who do all their day-to-day operations, even asking for loans, with cryptocurrencies through DeFi.

On the other hand, there are other professionals in the sector who believe that Bitcoin is the only real solution to the risks of CBDCs, especially if we focus on the loss of privacy of users because, as I mentioned in chapter 5, the characteristics of Bitcoin are different from those of most digital financial assets, including other cryptocurrencies, since it is decentralization at its best and its raison d'être is to be a store of value and not an investment asset.

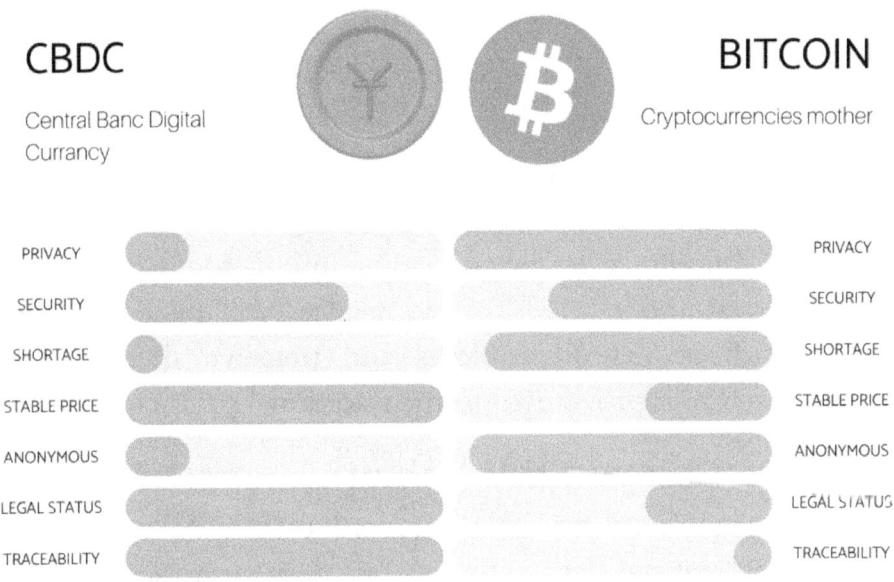

In fact, the creation of thousands of cryptocurrencies with no real value has led most people to view cryptocurrencies as assets to invest in due to their high volatility, but this is detrimental to Bitcoin, as it was not created to be a short-term investment, but a real complementary alternative to the traditional financial system and a real store of value.

In my opinion, Bitcoin is a different asset and has all the qualities discussed above, it is a very special asset and I think it has the potential to be a real alternative to CBDCs, but, at the same time, I think most people do not see Bitcoin in the same light, they see it simply as an asset for short term investment and that makes the above argument lose weight. In fact, for Bitcoin to develop to its full potential, it should be adopted on a mass scale, as the more people use it, the better these features develop. Bitcoin works in a similar way to mobile phones in the early days: having just one phone did not make sense, it is not useful, but nowadays, as everyone has a phone, it is a very important asset for us. It is the same with Bitcoin, if most people don't implement it or do it as a method of speculation, it will never be a real alternative to CBDC.

Moreover, most of the criticisms attributed to CBDCs can be attributed to the current FIATs, although perhaps to a lesser extent. Therefore, Bitcoin may be a real solution for total privacy advocates, but the rest of the population will probably adopt CBDCs without major problems and perceive them, out of ignorance, as an improvement to the traditional payment system.

Alex, what do you think then?

We have gone from the gold standard to the dollar standard, although the real standard is to generate debt without a standard. With the creation of CBDCs, central banks acquire too much power, much more than they currently have, and as is well known, when an entity has so much power over the future of the economy, it has absolute control over it and any mistake can be fatal for the world financial order.

A world without real liquidity, such as the one we are heading towards, is a world that owes itself much more than it has, something that will undoubtedly continue to increase due to the way the current financial system is designed and especially the future with the issuance of CBDCs. Excessively low debt and cash ratio generates socio-economic dependency, state aid and more debt as a consequence, and so on and so forth like a fish that bites its own tail.

In this sense, for film buffs, the instability that may be created is similar to that caused by 'the professor' in the last episode of the series, when he decides to take the entire national gold reserve of the Bank of Spain and exchange it for the same number of brass ingots without causing the absolute bankruptcy of the country.

In other words, the CBDCs will create money out of thin air without any real backing, the only backing will be the confidence we have in the central bank and that, like having brass ingots or chocolate biscuits, has no real tangible value.

In fact, in a report on CBDCs, the IMF explains the following:

'CBDCs are likely to have profound implications for monetary policy and financial stability. CBDCs could strengthen the usability, resilience and efficiency of payment systems and increase financial inclusion. However, if poorly designed, CBDCs could also lead to financial stability risks, data privacy and legal challenges, cyber risks and central bank operational risks. Moreover, the widespread use of CBDCs could change the configuration of the international monetary system. On the other hand, easy access to foreign CBDCs could generate risks of currency substitution and volatility of capital flows'.

In other words, even the IMF agrees with me!

CBDC technology allows central banks to exercise total control over the population, but, on the other hand, it also allows them to create a new totally digital financial system in which, technically, they can be used together with anonymous and private transactions, without being traceable. That is to say, depending on how they use the technology it will be benign or malignant for the interests of the citizen, for this reason, I am not saying that they are going to exercise total control over the population, I am saying that with CBDC they could do it and that, in my opinion, is enough, since we are totally dependent on the will of the central banks.

Finally, there is a phrase that I like very much and that I think defines me very much as a person: 'Fear ends where knowledge begins'. By this phrase I mean that it is good to have respect (not fear) for things we do not know, as long as they allow you to move forward, but if you make an effort and do some in-depth research on what you are afraid of, you will realize that it was not such a big deal. How many times have you been disproportionately afraid of something that really wasn't such a big deal?

That's why I encourage you to learn, especially on topics as relevant as the ones I've covered in the book and the ones I discuss with some of my personal finance clients. Don't be afraid of something before you know it, and if you are, remedy it through knowledge.

That is why I have written this book, because for us, ordinary citizens, it is going to mean a change, not very visible at first sight, but which may violate our most fundamental rights simply because of our lack of knowledge, so remember the phrase:

> "Fear end where knowledge begins."

Now, dear reader, comes the last part of the book and I have to say that it is not an indispensable part, I explain in a more technical way aspects related to CBDC technology and its impact. Therefore, feel free to finish the book if you think it is convenient, I only recommend reading it to that kind of reader who wants to learn about the technology behind it and who already has some previous knowledge on the subject.

NOTES

Dear reader, as I said, I recommend that you read this part only if you are really interested in any of the questions, i.e. this section is just a collection of questions that I have been asked over time and I think it can be useful.

Frequently asked questions (FAQ)
What differentiates a CBDC from a cryptocurrency?

As we have seen throughout the book, the main difference is that the former is created and regulated by a central bank and is therefore a legal tender, whereas a cryptocurrency is a decentralized asset.

Why are CBDCs to be created?

The main reason, according to most central banks, is that they are created to combat the weaknesses of cash. The reality is that the fight against fraud is one reason, but combating the rise of cryptocurrencies and, above all, eliminating cash is the main reason to be able to regulate and control transactions.

What will CBDCs change in terms of how they work for the citizen?

For the ordinary citizen it will be very similar to the financial system we live in today, as most payments are made by card or mobile phone. The most relevant changes are:

We will be able to have multiple accounts in one application.

We will be able to make payments offline and with the phone out of battery.

The cost of these advantages is that the central bank will have all the information about our transactions and our accounts available thanks to the blockchain.

Depending on whether they want to or not, they could infringe on our rights, putting expiry dates on our money, setting holding limits, etc.

How are they to be regulated?

They will be regulated by the central bank and the government of the country or region and are official legal tender.

What is the role of central banks in CBDCs?

Central banks have a major role, as they are the main actor in all transactions and have the upper hand.

Which CBDC is the most important?

Currently, the Chinese e-yuan is undoubtedly the most popular, both in terms of use cases and in terms of implementation and adoption.

Will they completely replace cash?

Yes, or at least that is the intention of central banks.

Bitcoin or physical gold?

Perhaps my opinion is a little different from most people, but if I have to choose, I choose Bitcoin for three reasons:

It is much easier to buy and sell and generates lower fees and transaction costs.

Maintenance, security and transportation costs are infinitely lower. Bitcoin can be stored in a cold wallet, and you can rest easy, whereas holding gold bullion is much more expensive and requires much more space.

Both are stores of value, but one of the most important values of a store of value is scarcity, and although both are scarce, new sources of gold can always be found, increasing the supply and affecting the price downwards, but new bitcoins will never be 'discovered'.

In fact, the history of gold is much longer than that of Bitcoin, but in the time that they have coexisted, the growth of Bitcoin has been much higher than that of gold, although in some ways this is normal, since the capitalization of one asset and the other is very different. However, despite its recent creation, it is already among the TOP10 most valuable assets in the world.

Is a bitcoin a blockchain?

No, a Bitcoin is not a blockchain.

Bitcoin: It is a digital currency or cryptocurrency that can be used to purchase goods, services or simply be held as a form of investment. Each Bitcoin is a digital token that has value and can be transferred between people.

2. Blockchain: This is the underlying technology that allows Bitcoin to exist and operate. The Bitcoin blockchain is a type of digital ledger that keeps track of all transactions made with Bitcoin. Every time someone sends or receives Bitcoin, that transaction is recorded in a block, and that block is added to a chain of previous blocks, hence the name 'blockchain'.

Why is the blockchain so secure?

The blockchain has several features that contribute to its security and reliability, but we focus on 3 now:

1. Encryption

- The blockchain uses advanced encryption techniques to protect information. Each transaction and block have a unique digital signature that is almost impossible to forge.

2. Decentralization

- Unlike centralized systems, where a single entity has total control, the blockchain is decentralized. Many computers (nodes) in different locations have a copy of the blockchain, and all must agree before a new block can be added. This reduces the risk of fraud and manipulation.

3. Consensus

- For a new block to be added to the chain, the nodes in the network must reach consensus, which usually involves solving a complex mathematical problem. This process, known as mining in the case of Bitcoin, ensures that only valid blocks are added to the chain.

What is encryption?

Bitcoin uses various encryption and cryptographic techniques to secure transactions and control the creation of new units.

1. Public Key Cryptography

- Bitcoin uses a public key cryptography system where each user has a pair of keys: a public key that acts as an address to which others can send bitcoins, and a private key that allows the owner of the key to access and spend bitcoins sent to that address.

2. SHA-256 hash (Secure Hash Algorithm 256)

- SHA-256 is a cryptographic hash function that takes an input and produces a fixed-length string of characters that appears random. Bitcoin uses SHA-256 to create addresses and form blocks on the blockchain.

3. Elliptic Curve Digital Signature Algorithm (ECDSA)

- ECDSA is the algorithm used to create a digital signature for each transaction. This signature proves that the transaction has been created by someone who has the private key corresponding to the public key (address) from which the bitcoins are being sent, without revealing the private key.

4. Proof of Work

- Although not an encryption technique per se, proof of work is a mechanism that requires miners to solve a complicated mathematical problem in order to add a new block to the blockchain, which provides additional security against attacks.

5. RIPEMD-160 algorithm

- RIPEMD-160 is another cryptographic hash function that is used together with SHA-256 to create a Bitcoin address from a public key.

These cryptographic techniques and algorithms work together to maintain the integrity and security of the Bitcoin system, ensuring that only the owners of bitcoins can spend them and that all transactions are verifiable and secure.

Do CBDCs use the same encryption methods?

The encryption and cryptography used in Central Bank Digital Currencies (CBDCs) may vary from one currency to another, as each central bank may opt for different technologies according to its specific needs and regulations.

What SHA-256 is?

SHA-256, which stands for Secure Hash Algorithm 256, is a cryptographic hash function that takes an input (or 'message') and returns a fixed string of 64 alphanumeric characters, regardless of the length of the input. The output, known as a hash, is unique for each unique input; even a tiny change in the input will produce a completely different hash. SHA-256 is designed by the US National Security Agency (NSA), and is widely used in various security applications, including data integrity verification and address generation on the Bitcoin network.

¿ How is a seed phrase technically generated?

Technically, the generation of a seed phrase involves the following steps:

1. Entropy generation: a random number of a certain length, which is the entropy, is generated.

2. Hashing: A hash function, such as SHA-256, is applied to create a checksum of the entropy.

3. Concatenation: The checksum is added to the end of the entropy.

4. Conversion: The concatenated entropy is divided into segments, and each segment is converted to a number.

5. Mapping: Each number is mapped to a word from a predefined list of words, known as a BIP-39 dictionary.

6. Seed Phrase: The selected words form the seed phrase, which can be used to generate private and public keys.

This process ensures that the seed phrase is unique and difficult to guess, providing a secure basis for key management in a cryptocurrency wallet.

Of these steps, which is the most important to make it unbreakable?

The most crucial step in making the seed phrase unbreakable is **Entropy Generation**. High entropy means that there is a large amount of randomness, which makes the seed phrase unpredictable.

If the entropy is low or if the random number generation process is weak, an attacker could predict or guess the seed phrase, compromising the security of the associated wallet.

Therefore, it is vital that entropy is generated in a secure and truly random manner to ensure the robustness of the seed phrase.

How does the seed phrase relate to the blockchain network?

The seed phrase is neither stored nor directly related to the blockchain. However, it is used to generate the private and public keys that allow users to interact with the blockchain. For example, sending and receiving cryptocurrencies, or interacting with smart contracts. Transactions made with these keys are recorded on the blockchain, but the seed phrase remains outside the chain, stored securely by the user. It is a crucial piece of information that connects users to their assets on the blockchain, allowing access to and control over their funds.

A clearer example of this interaction between the seed phrase and the blockchain.

Imagine that the blockchain is a huge locker with many compartments. Each compartment has a lock and can only be opened with a unique key. The seed phrase is like a magic machine that can make keys. When you enter your seed phrase into the machine, it gives you a key that you can use to open your compartment in the blockchain locker and access your stuff (like your Bitcoins).

If someone else has a different seed phrase, their machine will make a different key that will open a different compartment in the blockchain locker. That's why it's important to keep your seed phrase safe, because whoever has it can make a copy of your key and access your compartment in the blockchain.

But is a seed phrase a wallet?

No, a seed phrase is a set of words generated from a random number, which acts as the basis for creating the cryptographic keys (private and public) that are used in a cryptocurrency wallet. The wallet, on the other hand, is an application or device that manages these keys and allows interaction with the blockchain, such as sending or receiving cryptocurrencies.

1. Seed Token

   - Generated only once, when creating the wallet.

   - It must be stored securely, as it allows the keys, and therefore the funds, to be retrieved.

2. Wallet

   - Manages the keys generated from the seed phrase.

   - It allows to view the balance, receive and send cryptocurrencies.

The relationship is that without the seed phrase, you could not generate or retrieve keys from your wallet, and without a wallet, you could not manage or access your cryptocurrencies on the blockchain.

And where does the wallet keep the seed phrase to use it without knowing it or keeping it?

The wallets do not store the seed phrase after the keys have been generated. It is the user's responsibility to store the seed phrase in a safe place when creating the wallet. If the seed phrase is lost and the user does not have access to their wallet (for example, if the wallet is uninstalled or the device is lost), the funds stored in the wallet will be irretrievably lost. Therefore, it is crucial that users store their seed phrase in a safe place outside of their digital wallet.

Yes, but it uses the phrase seed, so it must have it somewhere?

The wallet uses the seed phrase to generate the cryptographic keys the first time it is set up, but it does not store the seed phrase for ongoing use. Instead, it saves the generated cryptographic keys. If you need to restore the wallet, for example, if you lose your device, you will have to provide the seed phrase again to regenerate the keys and access your funds. Therefore, it is crucial that you keep your seed phrase in a safe place apart from your digital wallet.

Will the same seed phrase trying to access balances with 2 different wallets generate the same public and private keys?

Yes, if you use the same seed phrase in two different wallets, the same public and private keys will be generated. This is because key generation is deterministic, which means that from the same input (the seed phrase) you will always get the same output (the keys). This allows you to restore and access your funds from any compatible wallet, as long as you have your seed phrase.

Is there a limit to the creation of seed phrases?

No, there is no practical limit to the number of seed phrases that can be created. The number of possible seed phrases is astronomically large due to the high entropy used in their generation. Although there is a theoretical limit based on the length of the entropy and the size of the word dictionary, this limit is so large that for all practical purposes, it can be considered that there is no limit to the number of seed sentences that can be created.

What is this mathematical calculation to validate a block?

The mathematical calculation you refer to is part of the 'mining' process in blockchain. To add a new block to the chain, miners must solve a complex mathematical problem, which is to find a value that, when applied to a hash function along with the block's data, produces a hash that meets certain criteria.

This process consumes time and energy, which helps protect the network by making it difficult for attackers to alter blocks once they have been added to the chain. It is also how miners earn new coins as a reward for their work.

While they are calculating that value, are they securing the network or is that calculation really of no practical use?

While the miners are calculating that value, they are contributing to securing the network. This calculation makes it difficult to alter the data of previous blocks, as any change would require recalculating the proof of work of all subsequent blocks, which is computationally infeasible. Moreover, by competing to solve the computation, miners deter potential attackers, as they would need an enormous amount of computational power to outperform all honest miners and alter the blockchain. Therefore, although it may seem like an arbitrary calculation, it is crucial for maintaining the integrity and security of the network.

Is it liking a way to seal the hash of the block?

Exactly, the mining process and the associated calculation act as a way of sealing the block. By solving the mathematical problem, miners are essentially creating a unique, verifiable seal that validates the block and its contents. This seal, once created, helps ensure that the block cannot be altered without redoing all the work, providing a crucial layer of security and integrity to the blockchain.

And if this value is found by only 1 miner, what happens to the other values found by the other miners, or do several miners have to find the same value at the same time?

When a miner finds the correct value that satisfies the requirements of the mathematical problem, and the new block is accepted by the network, the other miners must stop their work on the current block and start working on the next block. The values that the other miners had found for the previous block are no longer relevant. They do not need to find the same value; the first to find a valid value and have their block accepted by the network is the one who 'wins' the mining reward for that block. The other miners simply start working on the next block in the chain.

Could it happen that two miners find the valid value at the same time or within a very short time of each other?

Yes, it is possible for two miners to find a valid value for the mathematical problem at the same time or within a very short time of each other. This can lead to a situation known as a temporary fork in the blockchain, where there are two valid blocks competing to be added to the chain. The network will resolve this fork by continuing to build on the block that first receives the most confirmations from other miners, and eventually, one block will be accepted by the majority of the network while the other block will be discarded.

And even if one miner finds the value, the others will not accept it into the network if it does not meet certain requirements, correct?

Correct, even if a miner finds the value, the block must meet certain requirements and rules set by the network protocol to be accepted. The other miners and nodes in the network will verify the block before accepting it and continuing to build on it.

If the block does not comply with the rules, it will be rejected by the network, regardless of whether the miner solved the mathematical problem correctly. This helps maintain the integrity and security of the network.

What is the difference between a miner and a node?

A miner and a node are participants in the blockchain network, but they have different roles:

Miner:

Solves complex mathematical problems to validate and add new blocks to the blockchain.

They receive rewards for their work.

Node:

Maintains a copy of the blockchain and verifies the validity of transactions and blocks.

It does not receive direct rewards for maintaining the network but contributes to its security and decentralization.

All miners are nodes, but not all nodes are miners. Nodes without a mining function are known as full nodes.

What incentive does a node have to remain there if it does not receive rewards?

Nodes, while not receiving direct rewards like miners, have several incentives to participate in the network:

Security and Decentralization: They help keep the network secure and decentralized, which is beneficial to all participants.

Verification: They can verify transactions themselves without relying on third parties, which is useful for businesses or individuals who handle large amounts of cryptocurrencies.

Community Contribution: They contribute to the ecosystem and help maintain the integrity of the blockchain network, which can be ideologically motivated.

Additional Services: Some nodes can offer additional services to other users and receive revenue for it.

Do you have any further questions?

Leave me a review telling me what you thought of the book and ask me questions, I'll update the book with the latest news and add the best questions!

Acknowledgements

One of the most important qualities a person should have been to be grateful and, in fact, from my point of view, it is one of the keys to happiness.

Firstly, I would like to thank Mireia, my partner, who is always there for me in good times and bad, and I can assure you that she is not.

Secondly, to my father, who left us recently while I was writing the book and will never have the chance to read his son's work, and who I still find it hard to talk about without coming down on myself. Without a doubt, he left me the most beautiful thing a father can leave you, a legacy and an eternal pride.

Of course, to my mother, for always being there, for giving me life and for fighting for me like no one else has ever done.

Also, to the rest of my family, my brother, my nephews, my nieces and my nephews and others, because, as Michael J. Fox said, family is not something important, it is everything.

On the other hand, to my ex-professor and friend Marc Ricart Geli, who has been a key element in bringing this book to fruition, undoubtedly one of those people who inspire and who deserve to be recognized for his knowledge and his entrepreneurial spirit.

I can't forget Toni Trueba, a great friend and a crack at his job, also a vital part in making the aesthetics of the book as good as possible.

Lastly, I want to thank **YOU** for reading my first book and I hope that it has really helped you to learn about the money of the future.

Finally, I would like to ask you to rate my book and write a comment to express your opinion, thus helping me to reduce as much as possible the lack of knowledge about a subject that you now know will change the world economy, but which is still largely unknown.

www.ingramcontent.com/pod-product-compliance
Lightning Source LLC
Chambersburg PA
CBHW050310230526
45471CB00005B/2113